The Lie
of Global
Prosperity

How Neoliberals Distort Data to Mask
Poverty and Exploitation

by SETH DONNELLY

MONTHLY REVIEW PRESS
New York

Library of Congress Cataloging-in-Publication Data
Donnelly, Seth, author.
Title: The lie of global prosperity : how neoliberals distort data to mask
  poverty and exploitation / by Seth Donnelly.
Description: New York : Monthly Review Press, [2019] | Includes
  bibliographical references and index. | Identifiers: LCCN 2019028697 (print) |
LCCN 2019028698 (ebook) | ISBN
  9781583677650 (paperback) | ISBN 9781583677667 (cloth) | ISBN
  9781583677674 (ebook) | ISBN 9781583677681 (ebook other)
Subjects: LCSH: Poverty—Developing countries. | Neoliberalism. |
Capitalism—Moral and ethical aspects.
Classification: LCC HC59.72.P6 D66 2020 (print) | LCC HC59.72.P6 (ebook)
 | DDC 339.4/6091724—dc23
LC record available at https://lccn.loc.gov/2019028697
LC ebook record available at https://lccn.loc.gov/2019028698

Typeset in Minion Pro

MONTHLY REVIEW PRESS, NEW YORK
monthlyreview.org

5 4 3 2 1

Contents

Dedicated to my father, who stimulated my interest in global economics, introduced me to *Monthly Review*, and inspired me —and still does—to work for revolution

In systems organized upside down, when the economy grows, social injustice grows with it.—EDUARDO GALEANO, *OPEN VEINS OF LATIN AMERICA*

Preface

Anew era has been proclaimed. In recent years, we have seen one public figure after another come forward to announce a dramatic decline in global poverty. These heralds of a new age include Bill Gates, the World Bank, and a host of anonymous writers at *The Economist*. All bring the good tidings that capitalism—stoked by information technology and spread globally since the end of the Cold War—has ushered in a new epoch of shared human prosperity. The message bearers do not agree about everything: some cleave to neoliberal doctrine whereas others argue for a more statist, regulated economy. Yet all concur that current-day capitalism has spawned a new era of human redemption, and all believe that it combines economic development with a systematic reduction in poverty.

It would all be wonderful, if only it were true. In fact, capitalism in our time continues to produce distorted and stagnated development, and it goes on grinding down the majority of people. Yet the capitalist class and its allies work hard to make us think otherwise. They do so by spinning a web of spurious data, bad arguments, and sometimes outright lies. It's this class-based project, expressed in obscurantist claims about global prosperity, that this short book aims to debunk. The purpose is to expose the epidemic of poverty that is the real and persistent fruit of capitalist development.

In the arguments deployed here, I have tried to synthesize the findings of researchers from different fields into a work of popular education. The book's main audience is revolutionary activists and participants in social movements. In addition to bringing together previously disparate pieces of evidence, I have attempted to communicate the information in a clear, accessible manner. Along the way, I illustrate many of the more abstract findings with examples taken from my own experience as an activist.

In reporting on poverty in Third World countries (often called today the Global South), I try to show how global imperialist capitalism systematically produces poverty and subsequently attempts to cover up that crime with bad data and misleading arguments. The book does not directly address the interlocking forms of domination—national oppression, white supremacy, patriarchy, homophobia, xenophobia, ecocide, and others—that are key aspects of the same capitalist system. Nor does it deal with the grassroots and labor struggles that spring up throughout the world, resisting oppression and sometimes fighting to uproot exploitation once and for all. The methodological decision to leave such struggles outside the book's framework is not meant to discount their importance. On the contrary, the hope of overcoming global poverty depends on inter-movement solidarity and consolidating our collective capacities across borders into a revolutionary project. As Audre Lord declared some forty years ago, "The master's tools will never dismantle the master's house."

Note: The bulk of the research for this book was done between 2016 and 2017 in response to trumpeting by the World Bank and neoliberal trendsetters such as Bill Gates that global poverty had been dramatically reduced and that the corresponding United Nations Millennial Development Goal on poverty reduction had been successfully achieved in 2015. As such, this book does not address more recent developments, such as Trump's international economic policies, and the most recent data collected by international institutions. However, these more recent policies and data will not alter the fundamental findings presented here.

Many people have influenced my work in this book. Family, friends, and activists in social movements in which I have participated are all fundamental sources of inspiration. I also owe special thanks to John Bellamy Foster for initially encouraging this research, to Michael Yates and Chris Gilbert for their amazing editorial work, and to Martin Paddio and Susie Day at Monthly Review Press for helping shape and publicize this book. Finally, I owe thanks to Erin Clermont for her excellent copy editing.

Introduction: A New Millennium?

On February 29, 2004, one year after the United States invaded Iraq, an unnumbered aircraft bearing a U.S. flag flew out of Port-au-Prince. Inside were President Jean Bertrand Aristide and his wife. This was part of a carefully orchestrated regime change that Haitians refer to as the *coupnapping* of their democratically elected president.[1] In the months that followed, U.S. troops, together with their French and Canadian counterparts, began to occupy the Caribbean country. Meanwhile, a U.S.-backed "interim" regime systematically waged a war of repression against the country's poor majority, and especially against activists associated with Aristide's Fanmi Lavalas movement.

Following the coup, the U.S. government was able to secure a UN Security Council resolution establishing the Mission for the Stabilization of Haiti (MINUSTAH). "Stabilized" by UN "peacekeeping" soldiers (Blue Helmet troops), the interim government ramped up its reign of terror. UN troops began directly collaborating with the Haitian police in violent actions against civilians in popular, pro-Aristide neighborhoods such as Cité Soleil and Bel Air. Thousands were murdered, as bodies piled up in the streets and morgues, in what amounted to a systematic campaign to eliminate

Lavalas followers.[2] This human rights disaster was largely ignored by the international press.[3]

A public high school teacher in California's Bay Area, I was able to spend much of the summer of 2004 in Haiti, investigating prison conditions in Port-au-Prince as part of a small human rights team. We found the country's penitentiaries to be overflowing with political prisoners from the Lavalas pro-democracy movement. They were there together with random people from poor neighborhoods whose crime had been to be in the wrong place at the wrong time. The prison conditions were abysmal, far below the most basic human rights standards.

The next summer I returned to Haiti to continue this same work in prisons and also to participate in a Haitian labor movement conference. On July 6, a young Haitian journalist, activist, and friend—gaunt from malnutrition—tracked down our delegation with a view to sharing his video footage of a massacre by UN troops conducted earlier that morning in Cité Soleil, his own neighborhood. The next day, he skillfully guided me and a small team of Haitian human rights activists into this huge, pro-Lavalas community of approximately 300,000 people. At that time, the interim government and MINUSTAH had laid an all-out siege on Cité Soleil. The young journalist was clearly trusted by people of all ages who came forward to meet with us. His graceful way of relating to children, peers, and elders, combined with his energy to fight injustice, are still with me as I write this.

Once we got inside Cité Soleil, people came forward to tell us how MINUSTAH troops had surrounded, invaded, and fired indiscriminately into Cité Soleil, killing civilians. We saw bodies strewn on the ground, including those of twenty-two-year-old Sonia Romelus and her two children. Blue Helmet troops had shot and killed them in their home, according to the testimony of Romelus's surviving husband. Over the next forty-eight hours, our small team gathered comprehensive evidence that UN troops had carried out a massacre in Cité Soleil. We corroborated our eyewitness evidence with testimony from medical staff at the nearby Médecins Sans Frontières Hospital.[4]

On July 8, our team decided to confront the MINUSTAH high

command. They were working from the luxurious Hotel Montana, once a symbol of decadence under the Duvalier dictatorship. Inside the hotel, we managed to speak with Lt. General Augusto Heleno, head of the Blue Helmet mission, and Colonel Morneau about the events in Cité Soleil two days earlier. The two officers defended the MINUSTAH intervention, claiming that it was a successful anti-gang operation, targeting local leader Dread Wilme. They denied that the UN Peacekeeping Force had killed any civilians. Apparently, it was not worth their trouble to dispatch any investigators to Cité Soleil after the assault nor to the Médecins Sans Frontières Hospital that treated more than twenty civilians shot that day. To these MINUSTAH officials, it was simply an a priori truth that there had been no civilian victims.

We had to try another approach. During the fall of 2005, our team worked with volunteers from the National Lawyers Guild to file a legal complaint against the United States and Brazilian governments for their roles in facilitating MINUSTAH and police massacres in Haiti, especially in Cité Soleil. We submitted the complaint to the Inter-American Commission on Human Rights. There was, however, no response. Apparently, the crimes in Haiti's killing fields never happened, and the victims did not exist. The result was that MINUSTAH and the Haitian police would continue their lethal activities in total impunity.

Years later, in 2013, I was in Haiti with a delegation of my high school students. We got word that our friend, the journalist from Cité Soleil, had fallen ill. To check on him, a small group of us went into Cité Soleil. We eventually found him, lying on the dirt floor of a shack, obviously in pain, and with his feet extremely swollen. Pooling resources, we took him to a private hospital where he died several days later from an immunological breakdown. He was not yet thirty years old.

How could one describe his living conditions? Like so many in Haiti, he lived in a community without access to adequate water, electricity, sanitation, education, health care, employment, and food, among other necessities. He lived in a makeshift hovel and died young of a treatable illness. Yet World Bank opinion makers would deny that this man lived in poverty. That's because, with his sporadic income from courageous journalism and occasional remittances, he likely earned slightly more than $1.25 per day in Purchasing Power Parity (PPP) currency (in fact, far below $1.25 in U.S. hard currency). As such, his income would be above the World Bank's then prevailing International Poverty Line, and so he could figure in a statistic as part of the alleged decline in global poverty.

There is, in fact, a macabre coincidence between two parallel methods of record-keeping. On the one hand, the MINUSTAH high command erased the crime of their troops murdering people in Cité Soleil: the massacre never existed. On the other hand, the World Bank erases the crime of his poverty. It is this latter crime and its erasure—just as much a manifestation of imperialism as the *"coupnapping"* of Aristide and the MINUSTAH repression in its wake—that inspired this book.

IN SEPTEMBER 2000, the United Nations held the Millennium Summit, at which it set eight Millennium Development Goals (MDGs). The project went forward with the backing of all UN member states and an array of international organizations including the World Bank. The goals included: eradicating extreme hunger and poverty; achieving universal primary education; promoting gender equality and empowerment; reducing child mortality; improving maternal health; combating HIV/AIDS, malaria, and other diseases; ensuring environmental sustainability; and developing a global partnership for development. For each of the goals, the UN established targets and specified the international agencies responsible for monitoring progress.[5] The deadline for achieving them was 2015.

The Millennium Goals appear to be straightforward and wholly commendable. After all, who would object to eliminating extreme poverty, reducing hunger, and fighting disease? Yet closer examination reveals many shortcomings and contradictions in the MDG campaign. One basic problem is that the goals were never the result of a truly democratic procedure. The earlier UN practice of carefully drafting projects in committees, followed by extended debate in the General Assembly, was thrown by the wayside for this initiative. Instead, it was only the wealthy countries (those in the Organization for Economic Cooperation and Development (OECD)) that formulated the Millennial Goals. The role of other UN member states was simply to approve them by acclamation.[6]

It is ironic that OECD member countries should take it upon themselves to design a campaign against global poverty, since it is their own neoliberal policies and financial asphyxiation of the Third World that has led to so much poverty, hunger, and disease in the first place. That contradiction should itself give us pause, but it points to a second, even more serious problem: most solutions proposed for meeting the MDGs are actually geared toward extending and maintaining the same unfair global order. To confirm this, we need only consider the language about "partnerships" and "cooperation," which runs throughout the document. In effect, poor countries are supposed to cooperate with their imperialist masters in maintaining an unjust world order.[7]

It shows extremely bad faith that rich countries would propose to solve global poverty with this kind of campaign, when they could easily achieve all the basic goals established in the UN Millennium Declaration. In truth, the rich countries of the OECD would only have to spend— during one brief year—a small portion of their GDPs in reparations to Third World countries that were the victims of colonialism and neocolonialism. That alone would be enough to eliminate hunger and extreme poverty and establish universal access to decent water and sanitation, primary school education, and basic health care measures. In practice, however, rich countries have pursued exactly the opposite path. Not only have they given paltry assistance to poor countries, but much of that money is dedicated to repaying existing (unfair) debt or to funding the local military. More arms and more soldiers are just what is needed to eliminate poverty.

Of course, militarization is part of the problem, not part of the solution. By slightly cutting the United States' bloated military budget and diverting it to Third World countries, 17 million lives could be saved every year (not counting the lives saved by killing fewer people in war and occupation).[8] In the almost two decades since the UN's Millennium summit, that adds up to 300 million people who have died unnecessarily, a number greater than all the deaths in the Second World War. But militarism is too sacred to be affected by the Millienium Goals. So, the U.S. government goes on spending more than half of its discretionary fiscal budget on the military and, together with corporations such as Lockheed Martin, continues to function as the world's number one weapons dealer. The arms trade has devastating consequences. Even as I write, the people of Yemen face the threat of a huge famine as Saudi Arabia pulverizes their country with U.S.-supplied weapons.[9]

Leaving aside the Millennium campaign's many shortcomings and the bad faith of its architects, we must ask a simple question: Did this well-publicized and presumably worldwide campaign against poverty end in victory or defeat? The answer depends entirely on who is telling the story. In 2015, the UN issued its *Millennium Development Goals Report,* which declared an unequivocal victory in eradicating extreme poverty. Upon closer reading, however, one discovers that "eradicating extreme poverty" meant only *cutting in half* the proportion of the world's population living in that condition. The report also celebrated having reduced *by half* the percentage of undernourished people living in "developing countries."[10]

To fully answer the question of whether the campaign worked or not, we need to consider the UN's sources of data. In fact, both the data that the UN uses in the Millennium Goal campaign and its definition of extreme poverty come from the World Bank. When the campaign began in 2000, that institution defined extreme poverty as living on $1.25 per day or less. In 2015, the threshold was set at $1.90 per day. Looking back that year, the Bank observed an overall and ongoing reduction in extreme poverty:

The proportion of global population living on less than $ 1.90 a day in 2012 was about a third of what it was in 1990.... This confirms that the first Millennium Development Goal (MDG) target—cutting the extreme poverty rate to half of its 1990 level—was met well before its 2015 target date. From a broader historical perspective, the global poverty rate has fallen by approximately 1 percentage point a year since 1990, with rapid poverty reduction in China and India playing a central role in this outcome.

Based on this tendency, the Bank could forecast that "the number of people living in extreme poverty around the world is likely to fall to under 10 percent of the global population in 2015 giving fresh evidence that a quarter-century-long sustained reduction in poverty is moving the world closer to the historic goal of ending poverty by 2030."[11] The Bank credits economic growth fostered by neoliberal policies, especially as applied in China, East Asia, and India, for this impressive progress in eliminating poverty. According to this view, the global war against poverty may not be over, but victory is in sight.

Even as the world's population has grown the number of poor has gradually fallen. In 1990, almost 4 in 10 people were living under the international extreme poverty line of $1.90 a day. In 2013, that figure had fallen to just over 1 in 10. But that still represents more than 767 million people.[12]

Fewer People Live in Extreme Poverty Than Ever Before

World population in billions. Poor living below $1.90/day in 2011 PPP

■ Poor   Non-poor

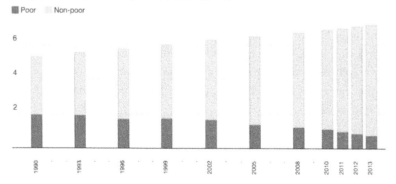

In keeping with this good news, the Bank's 2017 world income map presents a very positive picture of the global situation. Extreme poverty, it appears, is now confined to sub-Saharan Africa and parts of South Asia, such as Afghanistan and Nepal.[13]

The World Bank, a central source of information, relays its data on global poverty to the UN, nonprofit agencies, academics, and the media. For example, in 2016 the United Nations Development Programme (UNDP) issued a report titled *Human Development for Everyone* that relied on World Bank information to make these optimistic claims:

> The global extreme poverty rate ($1.90 a day) was estimated at less than 11 percent in 2013, a drop of more than two-thirds from the 35 percent in 1990. The decrease has been particularly remarkable in East Asia and the Pacific, where the proportion of people living on less than $1.90 a day fell from 60.2 percent in 1990 to 3.5 percent in 2013, and in South Asia, where the proportion fell from 44.6 percent to 15 percent.

Academics also build their arguments based on World Bank data. For example, in 2015 neoliberal economist Steven Radelet recycled World Bank poverty statistics to write *The Great Surge: the Ascent of the Developing World*, which argues that poorer countries are catching up to the richer ones, leading to global convergence.

In the print media, the Bank's information has become authoritative in part due to the lack of funding for investigative reporting. *The Economist* simply echoed Bank claims when it announced in 2013, in an issue titled "Toward the End of Poverty," that the global poverty rate had been "cut in half." The London-based magazine also gives a hearty second to the Bank's assertion that neoliberal globalization and the rise of capitalism in China are the principal engines driving these advances:

> The country that cut poverty the most was China, which in 1980 had the largest number of poor people anywhere. China saw a

huge increase in income inequality—but even more in growth. Between 1981 and 2010 it lifted a stunning 680 million people out of poverty—more than the entire current population of Latin America. This cut its poverty rate from 84% in 1980 to about 10% now. China alone accounts for around three quarters of the world's total decline in extreme poverty over the past 30 years.[14]

Within this broad consensus about declining poverty there is some squabbling about the reasons. *The Economist* downplays the role of aid, which "may have helped in some areas" but has little to do with "halving poverty." By contrast, the UNDP, the Gates Foundation, and Radelet all defend targeted international aid. Still, what is most remarkable is how all accept World Bank data and all coincide in embracing neoliberal globalization. Looked at closely, the general consensus on world poverty today is composed of three interrelated claims:

1. Extreme poverty is declining in the world, primarily due to neoliberal, capitalist globalization and rapid GDP growth in "developing" countries such as China and India.
2. The world is becoming more "flat," with "developing" countries catching up with the "developed" countries, implying a global convergence.
3. GDP growth should continue in order to achieve the World Bank's goal of "ending poverty by 2030," although the growth should be modified to make it is "sustainable" and not so environmentally destructive.

These ideas are hardly new. In fact, bourgeois ideologues have long argued that capitalism is a "rising tide that raises all boats." No doubt it is a comforting vision of the world if the boat you are in is a yacht. However, it obscures the truth about growing global poverty, inequality, exploitation, and environmental destruction. What is new today, however, is that the devastating consequences of capitalist expansion have become harder to hide, and the fairy tale about declining poverty needs to rely on increasingly sophisticated sleights-of-hand.

Each of these three hegemonic claims about world poverty is false. First, although capitalist globalization has generated rapid GDP growth in some Third World countries (growth that is now slowing down as First World economies stagnate), it has not contributed to a reduction of global poverty. If we use more accurate measures for poverty than those employed by the World Bank, then a very different, far more disturbing picture emerges. Second, there is ample evidence contradicting the "convergence" thesis and instead demonstrating expanding global inequality. Finally, the third claim, which brings in the idea of sustainability, is also false. While this book will not directly refute the third assumption of "sustainable growth" within a capitalist context, referrals will be made at the end to rigorous studies that effectively do.

PART ONE

GLOBAL POVERTY TODAY

Smoky Mountain in Manila, Philippines. Photo: Nigel Dickinson.
Nigel Dickinson, PhotoShelter

1. Problems with the World Bank's Poverty Metric

The headline of a 2015 World Bank press release reads: "World Bank Forecasts Global Poverty to Fall Below 10% for First Time." This seemed like great news, something indeed worth celebrating. But what did it mean in terms of income? The statement means that soon 90 percent of the world's population will live on $1.90 per day or more. This is the Bank's International Poverty Line, which enjoys great legitimacy worldwide. One might wonder how the Bank established $1.90 daily as the threshold for extreme poverty. The institution's publications reveal the basis for this figure to be surprisingly slim and arbitrary, based on doubtful reasoning and questionable data collection practices. A FAQ on the World Bank website explains the more or less circular procedure the Bank used to set the line:

> In 1990, a group of independent researchers and the World Bank proposed to measure the world's poor using the standards of the poorest countries in the World. They examined national poverty lines from *some of the poorest countries in the world*, and converted the lines to a common currency by using purchasing

power parity (PPP) exchange rates. The PPP exchange rates are constructed to ensure that the same quantity of goods and services are priced equivalently across countries. Once converted into a common currency, they found that in six of these very poor countries the value of the national poverty line was about $1 per day per person, and this formed the basis for the first dollar-a-day international poverty line.[15]

Remarkably, the World Bank's poverty line is based not on any direct and independent assessment of what people really need in terms of housing, food and clothing, but rather on *previously existing poverty lines* established by a minority of regimes in some of the poorest countries on the planet (only fifteen for the 2005 update to $1.25). Despite the Bank's periodic updating of its poverty line (for example, from $1.25 to $1.90 in 2015), this fundamental problem remains. It seems reasonable to suppose that an international poverty line that is not based on concrete data but on thresholds set by governments that may allow political motivations to influence their poverty standards might fall short of representing what people really need. This is indeed the case. In 2013, the United Nations Conference on Trade and Development (UNCTAD) admitted:

> The $1.25-a-day poverty line. . . *falls far short* of fulfilling the right to "a standard of living adequate for . . . health and well-being" (Universal Declaration of Human Rights, art.25.1) . . . Taking $5 as the minimum daily income which could reasonably be regarded as fulfilling this right, poverty would remain widespread even in those regions which might have largely or wholly eradicated extreme poverty [based on $1.25 per day] by 2030.[16]

Here we have an agency that is itself part of the UN recognizing the inadequacy of the standard threshold. Of course, figures such as $1.25 and $1.90 per day do indeed seem very low. But to get an understanding of just how low they are requires delving into the concept of purchasing power parity adjustments. Briefly, the upshot of purchasing power parity adjustment is that an income of $1.90 in the Bank's statistics does not refer to what a U.S. tourist can purchase if she exchanges that sum for local currency in a Third World country. It refers instead to the purchasing power of $1.90 inside the United States. As Dr. Jason Hickel, an anthropologist at the London School of Economics, points out, that makes the Bank's povertly threshold manifestly unreasonable:

> How much is $1.90 per day, adjusted for purchasing power? Technically, it represents the international equivalent of what $1.90 could buy in the United States in 2011. But we know that this amount of money is inadequate to achieve even the most basic nutrition. The U.S. Department of Agriculture calculates that in 2011 the very minimum necessary to buy sufficient food was $5.04 per day. And that's not taking account of other requirements for survival, such as shelter and clothing.
>
> We have many examples of this deficit. In India, children living at $1.90 still have a 60% chance of being malnourished. In Niger, infants living at $1.90 have a mortality rate three times higher than the global average. The same story can be told of many other countries. If $1.90 is too low to achieve basic nutrition, or to secure a fair chance of surviving the first year of life, why are we using it?[17]

In place of the Bank's $1.90 line, Hickel argues for a minimum that is much higher:

> If we want to stick with a single international line, we might use the "ethical poverty line" devised by Peter Edward of Newcastle University. He calculates that in order to achieve normal human life expectancy of just over 70 years, people need roughly 2.7 to 3.9 times the existing poverty line. In the past, that was $5 a day [same as UNCTAD]. Using the bank's new calculations, it's about $7.40 a day. As it happens, this number is close to the average of national poverty lines in the global south.[18]

As Hickel points out, the $1.90 per day standard is extremely low in relation to most national poverty lines. It is about one-fourth of the Third World average, and it is approximately *one-eighth* of the U.S. poverty line.[19] Since food can be just as expensive in Third World countries as in the United States, it is hard to see the reason for setting the line so low. Readers in the United States might consider that by the Bank's standards anyone earning $57 per month in our context would no longer be "extremely poor." Needless to say, living on that sum is almost unimaginable if we consider that it must cover *all* costs, including food, housing, and health care, and not just discretionary spending.

METHODOLOGICAL PROBLEMS OF THE BANK'S INTERNATIONAL POVERTY LINE

Household Surveys

The World Bank relies on "nationally representative household surveys" for its data on per capita income levels.[20] The problem with such surveys, which register either household income or consumption, is their sometimes arbitrary relation to people's real needs. On the one hand, some household surveys attach a monetary value to slum dwellings, which might boost a truly poor person above the official poverty line.[21] On the other hand, they sometimes overlook important, even life-saving subsidies and public services that people might receive.

These kinds of errors can lead to profoundly paradoxical outcomes. An especially clear case is how the free health care, education, and food that people receive in Mao's China do not enter into the calculation. As a result, Chinese people, who achieved new levels of food security and saw their life expectancy double in this period, were found to be on the whole "extremely poor." The Bank considers them to have been worse off than Haitians who might scrape together just over $1.90 daily by selling goods in the informal market or working in sweatshops. From the Bank's perspective, the Chinese only ceased to be "extremely poor" once they lost their collective lands, food rations, and medical care and began making iPhones and other export goods under atrocious conditions.[22, 23]

Purchasing Power Parity Conversion Factors

Setting an international poverty line requires comparing the purchasing power of different national currencies. Foreign exchange rates fail to solve this problem since they do not take into account local price structures. (A dollar won't buy you a haircut in New York but, exchanged for 70 rupees, it might do so in Delhi.) The International Comparison Program (ICP), started by the UN Statistical Division in 1968, sets the purchasing power parity rates that attempt to equalize the purchasing power of different national currencies. In principle, PPPs can be used to compare national incomes in a way more meaningful than market exchange rates.

The World Bank uses PPPs to set the international poverty line, and to update it so that the line allegedly reflects the same level of well-being in each country. The original dollar-a-day line, set in 1995 using PPPs from 1985, was updated to $1.08 in 1993 with PPPs from that year, and then was kicked up to $1.25 with the publication of new PPPs in 2005.[24] To date, the Bank's latest revision is $1.90 per day and is based on the 2011 PPP rates. Contrary to appearances, this new, nominally larger figure does not mean that the Bank raised the poverty threshold; in fact, setting it at $1.90 per day actually lowered the threshold, conveniently erasing 100 million poor people overnight.[25]

The Bank and the OECD use the PPP rates not just to set the extreme poverty threshold but also to compare different countries GDPs, attempting to adjust for the distorting effects of normal market exchange rates. The theory is that PPP rates can provide a statistical correction for the overvaluation or undervaluation—via prevailing market exchange rates—of national currencies that can inflate or deflate GDPs. By using the PPP rates, the ICP can better gauge the real size of the world economy. In the language of the ICP:

The ICP compares the gross domestic products (GDPs) of participating economies in real terms by removing the differences that are attributable to price levels and expressing the GDPs in a common currency . . . ICP comparisons of price and real expenditure levels of GDP are based on the expenditure aggregates of the national accounts using spatial price deflators or purchasing power parities (PPPs) as the measure of the price component. In these cases, the prices of products constituting final demand are collected and compared across economies to produce the price relatives, the PPPs, with which the GDPs and component expenditures being compared are deflated to obtain the real expenditure relatives.[26]

How does the ICP establish its PPP rates? It does so by collecting data on an internationally standardized "basket of goods and services." By comparing the prices of this standard basket in different national contexts, the ICP can establish the price ratios between comparable goods and services between countries. These indices are expressed through a common baseline international currency, which is the U.S. dollar.[27] As the ICP explained in its 2017 brochure:

Suppose that there is a basket of goods and services that costs 50 United States dollars (USD). 50 USD would be equivalent to 363 South African Rand (ZAR) when using a market exchange rate of 7.26. However, due to South Africa's lower price level in relation to the United States, the cost of a similar basket is actually 239 ZAR. Therefore, 50 USD would buy a larger basket of goods and services in South Africa than it would in the United States; the PPP of South Africa to the United States would be 239 ZAR/ 50 USD, which is equal to 4.77.

Interestingly, the PPP conversion factors between the United States and other OECD countries are often close to market exchange rates. Unlike the typical case when comparing rich and poor nations, the price structures of the former are similar.

The ICP next aggregates consumption patterns and priorities of people in both First World and Third World countries, thereby creating international "expenditure weights" within the basket, for example, food and services. Such aggregate weights, along with the PPP indices, are used to calculate the PPP conversion factors that determine the ratios of local currencies to the U.S. dollar. According to the Comprehensive Report by the World Bank Group of the 2011 International Comparison Program:

> PPPs are calculated in stages: first for individual goods and services, then for groups of products, and finally for each of the various levels of aggregation up to GDP. PPPs continue to be price relatives whether they refer to a product group, to an aggregation level, or to GDP. As one moves up the aggregation hierarchy, the price relatives refer to increasingly complex assortments of goods and services. Therefore, if the PPP for GDP between France and the United States is €0.95 to the dollar, it can be inferred that for every dollar spent on GDP in the United States, €0.95 would have to be spent in France to purchase the same volume of goods and services. Purchasing the same volume of goods and services does not mean that the baskets of goods and services purchased in both economies will be identical. The composition of the baskets will vary between economies and reflect differences in taste, culture, climate, price structure, product availability, and income level, but both baskets will, in principle, provide equivalent satisfaction or utility.[28]

The PPP rates are based on the reference year in which the ICP published the latest PPP indices between goods and services within the basket. The most recent reference year is 2011. Despite the reasoning behind PPP conversion factors, it is doubtful that their use is any less arbitrary than employing normal market exchange rates in international poverty assessments or GDP comparisons. Using PPP conversion factors means that if the price of a significant commodity such as housing is particularly high or low in the base country (the

United States) in the reference year, this will influence the PPP conversion factors with other countries.

The upshot of PPP conversions is that the "dollar a day" poverty line really gravitates around a half or a third of a dollar for many countries. This is because, even if the U.S. dollar serves to establish the Bank's international poverty line, the dollars referred to are *not* based on what the dollar can purchase in a foreign country via normal market exchange rates. Instead, the basis is the amount of a country's currency that when *used locally* would have the same purchasing power as a dollar in the United States. The 2016 *market exchange rate* between the U.S. dollar and the Haitian gourde was approximately 1:63. Using this exchange rate, the current $1.90 poverty line would be equivalent to living in Haiti on about 120 gourdes per day. This is insufficient for survival, since it falls far short of the costs of securing nutrition, housing, transportation, energy, education, health care, clothing, cooking utensils, among other necessary goods in Haiti. Yet because of the PPP conversion rates, the Haitian poverty line comes far short of even 120 gourdes daily. This is because the $1.90 per day benchmark is based on PPP exchange rates (conversion factors) that are consistently and significantly lower between the United States and Third World currencies than prevailing market exchange rates.[29] In fact, comprehensive research has found that "the poorer the country, the lower will be the exchange rate value of its currency in relation to the PPP value of its currency."[30]

Returning to Haiti, the 2016 PPP conversion factor between the dollar and the gourde, based on "private consumption," was 1:28. This meant that for every 28 gourdes a Haitian had, he or she in theory had $1(PPP). In contrast, the official exchange rate in 2016 was approximately 1:65.[31] By using the PPP ratio, the World Bank statistically elevated by more than 100 percent the dollar incomes of Haitians, thereby artificially reducing poverty. Using this PPP conversion factor for the $1.90 poverty line, it would seem that Haitians would need only 54 gourdes per day in Haiti in order to avoid extreme poverty. Given that the official exchange rate is now over 1:70 and many products Haitians need to buy, including foods, are imports from the

United States—at even marked-up prices—the 54 gourdes poverty
line is beyond absurd.

As Aseem Shrivastava wrote in 2006, the conversion of local currencies into U.S. dollars via PPP conversion factors is done by "taking
into account the lower cost of living in impoverished countries" and
applying a "conversion factor" to the "market exchange rates to calculate what is minimally necessary to survive there." He further adds:

> Using widely quoted World Bank numbers on GDP, this conver-
> sion factor for a country like India (2005) can be computed to
> be approximately 5.3 [PPP ratio of Indian rupees to U.S. dollar].
> This means that $1.08 a day in India should effectively imply a
> purchasing power of about 20 cents a day. . . . Given how the
> numbers are quoted everywhere, the dominant impression that
> is conveyed is that the poor are living on less than $1 or $2 a day
> when, in fact, it would be enormously more accurate, as far as
> everyday English is concerned, to say that the poor are living on
> less than $0.20 or $0.40 a day.[32]

In other words, when the $1.90 per day is reconverted back into the
currencies of Third World countries such as India via the PPP conversion formula, it is actually worth considerably less than $1.90 (if
it were exchanged and spent in the Third World country). To determine this PPP conversion factor for each country's currency into PPP
dollars, the ICP collects data on the prices of many different goods
and services in that country in reference to their costs in the United
States. These data are used to create an international standard or "general consumption" basket. If the goods and services in a poor country
such as India are, for example, one-third as expensive as such goods
and services in the United States, the PPP conversion factor from
Indian rupees into the U.S. dollar is a ratio of 3:1. Nobel Prize–win-
ning economist Angus Deaton explains the reasoning:

> Non-traded goods are typically cheaper in poorer economies,
> so that PPPs are typically lower than exchange rates for poor

countries, and are more so the poorer the country: for example, in 2011 the market exchange rate for India was 46.7rupees to the dollar, while the PPP exchange rate for consumption was 15.0 rupees to the dollar.[33]

In other words, $1.90 PPP is actually the equivalent of approximately 63 U.S. cents based upon the presumed differences in cost of living between India and the United States. If we properly adjust for the PPP conversion factor, it might be more accurate to say that the Bank is celebrating the reduction of extreme poverty in the world based on more people living on more than, say, an average of 60 cents a day in poor countries today, instead of $1.90 (PPP).

To show how questionable the Bank's data can be, using the $1.25 benchmark PPP, the Bank placed the "extreme poverty" rate in India at slightly above 30 percent in 2007.[34] The government of India reached a similar, official poverty estimate of 26 percent, based on the number of people living on less than 12 rupees per day, that is, about 30 U.S. cents in 2007.[35] (It is safe to assume that the Indian government had simply set its official poverty line as equivalent to the Bank's $1.25 standard, that is, 12 rupees per day when applying the relevant PPP conversion factor at that time.) In contrast, the Indian state-run National Commission for Enterprises in the Unorganised Sector (NCEUS) issued a 2007 report that reached very different conclusions. Instead of using 12 rupees as the poverty line, NCEUS used 20 rupees (50 cents) and found that 77 percent of Indians—836 million people—live in poverty in conditions that, in the report's words, "are utterly deplorable."[36]

The report further argues that those below the poverty line must generally coincide with the informal sector (what Marx called the "reserve army of the unemployed"):

One of the major highlights of this Report is the existence and quantification of unorganized or informal workers, defined as those who do not have employment security, work security and social security. These workers are engaged not only in the unorganized sector but in the organized sector as well. This universe of informal workers now constitutes 92 percent of the total workforce. We have also highlighted, based on an empirical measurement, the high congruence between this segment of the workforce and 77 percent of the population with a per capita daily consumption of up to Rs. 20 (in 2004–05) whom we have called "Poor and Vulnerable." The number of persons belonging to this group increased from 811 million in 1999–2000 to 836 million in 2004–05.[37]

The core finding of this report is a well-documented increase in poverty—up to 836 million people by 2004–05—precisely at a time when the Bank claims Indian poverty rates are falling. Not surprisingly, the report's findings, because they are based on an analysis of the country's concrete reality rather than abstract Bank parameters, jibe with the claims of Indian intellectuals such as Arundhati Roy, Jayati Ghosh, Rahul Goswami, C. P. Chandrasekhar, and Prabhat and Utsa Patnaik.[38] What the country's neoliberal government and the World Bank have in common is a desire to avoid the realities of true poverty. Unfortunately, reducing poverty by fiat is not done in India alone but rather among many overeager governments aspiring to chalk up impressive but doubtful progress in reaching the UN's Millennial Goals.

PPP Conversion Factors Reduce Poverty Counts by Underestimating Food Costs for the Poor

Over the past twelve years, I have made more than twenty trips to Port-au-Prince, where I worked shoulder to shoulder with Haitian grassroots activists. As a result of this on-the-ground solidarity work, I can testify as to how absurd the Bank's claim is that people earning more than $1.90 in PPP dollars are no longer "extremely poor." In April 2008, our trip came in the wake of the food riots that erupted in Port-au-Prince over rising food prices. An article in *The Guardian* reported on the dire situation in the island:

Food prices have risen 40% on average since the middle of last year, causing unrest around the world, with riots seen in countries such as Burkina Faso, Cameroon and Egypt. For months, Haitians have compared their hunger pains to "eating Clorox [bleach]" because of the burning feeling in their stomachs.[39]

This was also the year that some impoverished Haitians resorted to eating dirt cookies to alleviate their hunger pangs.[40] Nevertheless, if these same Haitians were earning more than 50 cents a day in the informal sector, they would not have qualified as "extremely poor" by the World Bank's standards.

Food is one of the most basic human necessities, and when it becomes costly or inaccessible the effects will be felt rapidly among the poor, who often spend most of their income on food. Food prices began to rise in 2002, as a result of agribusiness tightening control of the world's food system.

Since the World Bank had earnestly promoted agribusiness in the 1970s in the name of "development," perhaps it is not surprising that it tends to minimize the destructive impact of rising food prices on the world's poor. As John Smith observed:

The very sharp increases in food and fuel prices beginning in 2002 . . . signify that current PPP indices significantly exaggerate the real purchasing power exercised by low-wage workers in both rich and poor countries.[41]

Because the PPP expenditure weights within this international "basket of goods and services" are aggregates of consumption patterns in both poor and rich countries, they underemphasize the real expenditure weight of food to poor people throughout the Third World. This is because food, including basic grains, is far cheaper relative to the costs of other goods and services in rich countries than in Third World countries. As Sanjay Reddy and Thomas Pogge noted in their detailed 2005 critique of the Bank's methodology, the prices of food and basic grains are far higher than suggested by the PPP conversion factor for general consumption . . . In the vast majority of low-income countries, food prices are again higher [in the 1993 benchmark year] than consumer prices in general—27% higher on average (31 percent higher when weighted by the population). Bread-and-cereals prices are on average 51 percent higher (40 percent higher when weighted by population) than consumer prices in general. By any reasonable judgment, these magnitudes are very substantial, suggesting that using a more appropriate PPP concept would greatly increase the estimated extent of severe income poverty worldwide.[42]

Sanjay Reddy and Rahul Lahoti update this critique in their 2016 article "1.90 a Day: What Does It Say?" Here they contrast the Bank's $1.90 poverty line with the U.S. Department of Agriculture's 2011 calculation of the minimum cost achieving the "recommended dietary allowances," known as the "Thrifty Food Plan." For a family of four with two children that already has a kitchen and cooking utensils, the USDA found that $5.04 per person per day was needed to afford minimum food requirements. The plan did not take into account other costs essential to survival, such as transportation, rent, clothing, and health care. It must be kept in mind that the Bank's $1.90 standard is based on the alleged income required to avoid extreme poverty in the United States. This standard is then translated into local currencies in other countries through PPP conversion factors. How can someone avoid extreme poverty in the United States on $1.90 per day if this is roughly a third of what the USDA calculates a person needs just to meet elementary nutritional requirements? Reddy and Lahoti examined global poverty trends between 1980 and 2012 by using the $5.04 standard and a standard at half of its value, $2.52, applying the "general consumption" PPP conversion factors used by the Bank and "food" PPP conversion factors more appropriate to Third World realities. Their findings are a stark rebuttal of the Bank's rosy prognosis that "extreme poverty" has fallen by half during the new millennium.

Selecting the Thrifty Food Plan's allowance as an IPL [International Poverty Line] leads to a substantial increase in poverty headcount ratios, both globally and across all regions. If general consumption PPPs are used, more than 80 percent of people in South Asia and sub-Saharan Africa are found to live below the line of $5.04 per day. Even if only half the U.S. level is used, the poverty headcount ratio nearly doubles [from the Bank's "extreme poverty" estimates] in East Asia and South Asia. Using more appropriate food PPPs increases the poverty rate across all regions; 90 percent of South Asians consume below the Thrifty Plan level.[43]

For both general consumption PPPs and food PPPs, if $5.04 is used as the standard, the absolute numbers of people considered "extremely poor" has increased significantly since 1980 and is still above 1990 levels, despite very limited minor declines in more recent years.

PPP Conversion Factors Reduce Poverty Counts by Overemphasizing Services

While the ICP's mythical "basket of goods and services" underestimates the expense and centrality of food to the poor, "services" are overemphasized and given disproportionate expenditure weight because they account for so much consumption in rich countries. By privileging services as an expenditure weight, this artificially inflates the alleged purchasing power of poor people in Third World countries where services, in contrast to food, are often dramatically cheaper than in rich countries. As the service sector continues to grow in First World economies, and services remain markedly cheaper in Third World economies, PPP conversion factors automatically and artificially reduce poverty headcounts in the Third World by boosting alleged Third World purchasing power over services that are not essential (unlike food) to the survival of poor people. Reddy and Pogge showed how this problem affected mathematical methods (EKS and G-K systems) widely utilized in the construction of PPPs:

Consider services, which tend to be (relative to other commodities) expensive in rich countries and cheap in poor ones. The more money is spent (notably in rich countries) on services, the stronger an impact [aggregate weight] prices for services have on calculated PPPs. In this way, high prices for, and high consumption of, services in rich countries lower the calculated PPP of the currency of all poor countries, thereby lowering their apparent price levels, national poverty lines, and poverty headcounts.[44]

In 2006, the ICP acknowledged this problem with the "standard basket" or "general consumption" PPPs:

> In the absence of poverty-specific PPPs, the common practice is to use PPPs for aggregate consumption. This has two limitations. First, the PPPs are based on price consumption items for all countries in comparison. Consequently, the PPP estimates for developing countries are unduly influenced by the consumption baskets and spending habits of their developed counterparts. Second, the PPPs are derived using national expenditure weights. Therefore, goods that are important to the poor and comprise a large part of their expenditure carry proportionally less weight.[45]

Or, as Reddy and Lahoti more recently put it, "Under the current method, data on Japanese real-estate prices may impinge on whether a household in India is deemed to be living in extreme poverty or not."[46]

Problems with the World Bank's Recent Use of Sectoral PPPs

The Bank's data on extreme poverty reduction also depends upon the efforts by Bank economists to estimate and use intra-country "sectoral PPPs," that is, alleged differences in prices between urban and rural areas within China, India, and Indonesia. The Bank did not carry out such analysis in other large Third World countries such as Nigeria or densely populated ones such as Bangladesh. Certainly, it makes sense to attempt to account for price differentials facing urban and rural households, but the Bank's methods of determining these differentials are open to serious criticism. Among other issues, the Bank

> assumed for India (and followed a parallel procedure for other countries), firstly, that the ratio of rural to urban prices, and thus of sectoral PPPs, could be derived from the ratio of previously defined rural and urban poverty lines; and secondly, that the national price level was a weighted average of the (unknown) rural and urban price levels, with the number of price points sampled by the ICP in its national PPP-determination exercise defining the weights.[47]

With India, the Bank adopted rural and urban poverty lines that were so unrealistic that they were even rejected by the neoliberal Indian government. Consequently, by using these lines, the Bank effectively erased much of rural poverty in India and arrived at the absurd proposition that the difference between rural and urban price levels was 51 percent, even though the ICP estimated the difference to be only 3 percent. As Reddy and Lahoti commented on the Bank's methods in India, as well as China and Indonesia:

> It is not only paying attention to sectoral variation that matters, but also which method of inter-sectoral adjustment is used. The Bank's chosen approach leads to the most optimistic portrayal of rural purchasing power, and thus of the rural [poverty] head-count. . . . Estimates of global poverty levels are thus enormously affected by this single, very questionable choice. Using ICP national PPPs for China, India, and Indonesia would substantially increase their poverty rates, raising the estimated number of poor people in the world on 2011 figures by an additional 290,000,000. The trend-rate of global poverty reduction from 1990 to 2011 also appears more favorable using the sectoral PPPs the Bank's economists have chosen in the recent period.[48]

*General Consumption PPPs Do Not Effectively Address the Role of
Capital and Intermediate Goods in the Fight Against Poverty*

In his 2008 essay "The Poverty of Statistics," Alan Freeman addressed another problem with the "general consumption" PPPs used by the World Bank in its poverty estimates. These PPPs understated the high price of "capital goods" and omitted the high prices of "intermediate goods" for Third World countries; that is, the PPPs did not effectively incorporate the costs of machinery, equipment, technology, and other inputs necessary to industrial and high-tech production. These goods are typically much more expensive in the Third World, since many are imported from the First World and marked up; for example, Portland cement was imported into Haiti. Though marginalizing the impact of these goods' prices on consumption PPPs may seem to make sense since poor people do not eat cement, such statistical marginalization obscures the ongoing neocolonial dependency of Third World countries on the rich nations for these goods. This dependency continues to undermine the capacity of Third World countries to authentically develop their own economies, produce on their own terms, and overcome poverty. Moreover, the high price of such goods can immediately and directly burden poor people; with the high price of cement in Port-au-Prince, it is more expensive for people to build their own homes, as so many of the poor attempt to do. Freeman warned:

> The divergence between the price of consumer and capital goods [for the Third World] has been accentuated massively under FTL [Financial and Trade Liberalization], leaving many parts of the South dependent on a relation to the North as distorted as in the classical period of neocolonialism. . . . With the post-liberalization closing of the scissors, and the onset of a new period of rising consumer good prices as yet unaccompanied by reductions in the price of capital and intermediate goods, hundreds of millions of people are now at risk on a scale no statistic can conceal.[49]

PPP Conversion Factors Understate and Misrepresent
Global Inequality

Just as PPP conversion factors exaggerate the purchasing power of the poor in the Third World, thereby artificially reducing poverty headcounts in the World Bank's data, these conversion factors also exaggerate the GDP per capita of Third World countries, thereby giving an appearance of falling global inequality. When PPP conversion factors are applied, the GDP per capita of Third World countries as a share of GDP per capita of rich countries rose from just under 13 percent in 1960 to just under 18 percent in 2008. However, if PPP conversion factors are jettisoned in favor of normal market exchange rates converted into the U.S. dollar, the GDP per capita of Third World countries as a share of that of First World countries fell from just under 18 percent in 1960 to about 15 percent in 2008. Using normal exchange rates, if China is excluded, the Third World share fell from just under 10 percent in 1960 to about 6 percent in 2008.[50] Both global poverty and inequality are obfuscated by PPP conversion factors. Since international trade is based on official exchange rates—rates that continue to disadvantage Third World countries with deteriorating terms of trade, with low prices for Third World exports and high prices for imports from First World countries— the use of mythical PPP factors understates the problem. Likewise, since people in the Third World depend upon overpriced imports from First World countries (for example, Haitians must buy imported U.S. rice) based upon official exchange rates, the use of PPP factors exaggerates the purchasing power of poor people in the Third World.

The World Bank's IPL Updates Are Unreliable

Reddy and Lahoti have extensively deconstructed the myth of temporal reliability and consistency shrouding the Bank's updates to its international poverty line, most recently from $1.25 (based on 2005 PPP conversion factors) to $1.90 (based on 2011 PPP conversion factors). In response to the question of whether the purchasing power of the 2011 IPL corresponds to that of the 2005 IPL, these authors responded:

> Unfortunately, it does not. This is because when the 2005 IPL is translated into local currencies, and then updated using the consumer price indices (CPIs) of the individual countries [adjusting accurately for inflation or deflation], this leads to amounts of local currency in 2011 values which are generally very different from those implied by converting any given IPL directly using the 2011 PPPs.[51]

Aside from the fact that the Bank's 2005 IPL of $1.25 per day was far below the requirements of human survival and development, the update of this $1.25 line must be interrogated. If the $1.25 line was updated by accounting for domestic price fluctuations in individual countries, the Bank in 2015 would have reached a different IPL and poverty headcounts than it did by using 2011 PPP conversion factors.

The World Bank Has Assumed that Economic Growth Automatically Reduces Poverty

Just as greater consumption of more expensive services and poverty-irrelevant commodities in the First World has given the false appearance of poverty statistically falling in the Third World through the Bank's reliance on hypothetical PPPs, so too has "economic growth" provided an illusion of poverty falling. This is because the Bank has assumed that as "mean consumption," that is, the new "average" level of consumption income, rises with growth, poverty must therefore be falling.[52] However, this "trickle-down" assumption is clearly not logical; if 10 percent of a country's population sees a surge in incomes, boosting overall economic growth and the "mean" of "consumption" in the country, it does not follow that the bottom 90 percent is experiencing poverty reduction. Many could experience greater levels of poverty, just as the environment can be suffering from more destructive externalities, as happened in Brazil during its "economic miracle" under the military dictatorship. The only way to determine if growth is in fact trickling down is through more comprehensive surveys of poor households, but these surveys have not been conducted as rigorously and frequently as required.

THIS IS A LIMITED SAMPLE of the many problems the World Bank's methods in measuring global poverty and identifying trends over time create.[53] Laying bare the absurdity of the Bank's contrived statistical universe was the *Financial Times* headline on September 23, 2015, "Earth's Poor Set to Swell as World Bank Moves Poverty Line." This was based on a proposed IPL of $1.92 that would have resulted in 148 million more "extremely poor" people in the world. The Bank soon revised the IPL down to $1.90 and avoided this embarrassing predicament.[54] And so it is that 2 cents on the U.S. dollar, PPP-adjusted, saved the world from the debacle of a surge in extreme poverty.

THE WORLD BANK'S DATA ON POVERTY AT FACE VALUE

But aside from methodological concerns, what does the Bank's current data on poverty, *taken at face value*, really show? Does the Bank's own data substantiate its good-news headlines? The Bank's data was carefully analyzed by the Pew Research Center, which issued a 2015 report titled *A Global Middle Class Is More a Promise Than a Reality*. The report notes the Bank's data showing that the number of people living below $1.90 PPP per day (the report rounds up to $2 PPP per day) fell by 669 million people between 2001 and 2011, that is, from 29 percent to 15 percent of the world's population. However, the number of so-called low-income people (with between $2 and $10 PPP per day) increased during the same period by 694 million, from 50 percent to 56 percent of the world's population. Most of these low-income people are living below the $5 UNCTAD or Ethical Poverty Line requirement to meet basic needs ($7.40 today using the 2015 updated $1.90 PPP benchmark). "Globally, the majority of people live on about $3 a day," Rahesh Kochhar, associate director at Pew, said in the report.[55] As Jason Hickel shows in his research, using Bank data, the ranks of people living below this $5 per day threshold grew by about 1 billion from 1980 to the present and now includes 4.3 billion people, more than 60 percent of the world population.[56] Taken together, as the Pew report documents, 71 percent of the world's population is in the low-income category, with most living in severe poverty.

> Most low-income earners in 2011 lived closer to the poverty line ($2 per day) than the threshold for middle-income status ($10 per day). Indeed, in both 2001 and 2011, living on either $1–2 or $2–3 per day was the most probable outcome, globally speaking. Overall, in both years, the vast majority of people live on less than $10 per day.[57]

As indicated by its title, the Pew report makes clear that an ascendant global middle class is more a "promise than reality." The report defines "middle class" as those living on between $10 and $20 PPP per day. The report observes that in "the 111 countries included in this study, 783 million residents were middle income in 2011, compared with 398 million in 2001. Thus, the middle-income population—those living on $10–20 per day—nearly doubled, increasing by 386 million in the first decade of the new century." However, this was only half the increase of the number of those living between $2 and $10 per day. By 2011, the global middle class represented only 13 percent of the world population. More than half of this increase came from the growth of China's middle class. "By 2011, the share of China's population that is middle income stood at 18% in 2011—up by 15 percentage points from 3% in 2001. In absolute terms, 203 million people in China crossed the middle-income threshold of $10 per day from 2001 to 2011." The growth of the super-rich in China also contributed to an increase in the global upper class, even though the vast majority of the Chinese people remain "low income," making China today one of the most unequal societies on the planet. As *Bloomberg News* reported in early 2012:

The net worth of the 70 richest delegates in China's National People's Congress . . . rose to $89.8 billion in 2011, a gain of $11.5 billion from 2010. . . . That compares to the $7.5 billion net worth of all 660 top officials in the three branches of the US government.[58]

Meanwhile, "the middle class barely expanded in India and Southeast Asia, Africa, and Central America."[59]

The term "middle class" is also misleading. When the adjustment is made for the PPP conversion factor, living on $10 to $20 PPP per day is, roughly speaking, more like living on anywhere between $3 and $7, converted into local currencies. This is far below the U.S. poverty line of $15.77 per person per day. As the report acknowledges, "Even those newly minted as middle class enjoy a standard of living that is modest by Western norms." Indeed, the deception about a new middle class sweeping the world is akin to the deception about the "end of poverty" line advanced by the World Bank and *The Economist*. An example of such deception is a 2011 report by the African Development Bank—a relative of the World Bank and strongly influenced by the U.S. and OECD governments—that claimed the African middle class had grown over the past two decades to include 33 percent of the African population, representing a dramatic reduction in poverty. However, as Martin Hart-Landsberg reveals:

> The problem with this celebration of the African experience is that it is largely a figment of clever marketing. The African Development Bank defined the middle class as those with a daily consumption of between $2 and $20 PPP. . . . It turns out, according to the African Development Bank statistics, that 61% of Africans still live below the $2 [PPP] a day poverty line. Approximately 21% more live just above that amount, between $2 and $4 [PPP] a day. The Bank, while including them in the middle class, also calls this cohort a "floating class." . . . In other words, after a sustained period of rapid growth, more than 80% of Africa's population still struggles with poverty.[60]

The Pew report contains a graph that vividly illustrates how the overwhelming majority of the world's people are essentially poor and how close so many of those who have escaped the $2 PPP line still remain close to that line, just as so many who have crossed the $10 PPP line still remain close to that line.

Clearly, neoliberal, capitalist globalization is failing to spread prosperity to the world's people. It takes a great deal of effort to intellectually and ethically justify this system, particularly in light of the extractivist/ecocidal GDP growth alongside the human oppression fueling its expansion. An example of how such efforts reach the level of absurdity is found in the following passage in Steven Radelet's *The Great Surge: The Ascent of the Developing World*:

> In 1981 the extreme poor lived on an average of just $.74 [PPP] a day [based on World Bank data]. . . . By 2010, the average was $.87 [PPP} a day. . . . This change is hardly a huge increase— about 18% . . . but neither is it stagnation.[61]

Further down on the same page, Radelet clarifies that "people are not yet rich." Indeed.

2. Other Metrics and Dimensions of Global Poverty

The Multidimensional Poverty Index

Apart from the World Bank's income metric, what other ways of measuring global poverty are there? An interesting indicator is the Multidimensional Poverty Index (MPI), developed in 2010 by the Oxford Poverty and Human Development Initiative and the UNDP. The MPI does not focus on income but on deprivations in the areas of health, education, and living standard. Within these three categories are a series of weighted indicators. For example, the category of *living standard* breaks down into indicators dealing with cooking fuel, sanitation, drinking water, electricity, floor type, and assets. A person is considered poor if deprived of at least one-third of the weighted indicators.[62]

Using this methodology, the 2017 MPI finds that "a total of 1.45 billion people from 103 countries are multidimensionally poor. . . 26.5% of the people."[63] Some of these countries are middle- to high-income, so the percentage of multidimensionally poor is considerably higher if they are removed from the picture. For example, in South Asia, 41.6 percent of the population is MPI poor, which is more than twice the World Bank's rate of extreme poverty for that region. In sub-Saharan Africa, multidimensional poverty affects 60.1 percent of the population, a rate one-third higher than the $1.90 per day standard yields.[64] The 2017 MPI report also demonstrates the disproportionate impact of poverty on children:

> Half of all multidimensionally poor people—48%—are children. Nearly two out of every five children—37%—are multidimensionally poor. This means 689 million children are living in multidimensional poverty. Most MPI poor children live in South Asia (44%) and in sub-Saharan Africa (43%). In 36 countries, including India, at least half of all children are MPI poor. In Ethiopia, Niger and South Sudan over 90% of children are MPI poor. Half of MPI poor children live in "alert"-level fragile states, and child poverty levels are the highest in the worst of the fragile states. Two-thirds of poor children live in middle-income countries. Poor children are on average deprived in 52% of weighted indicators.[65]

Based on concrete deprivations, the MPI paints a much more disturbing picture of global poverty than the World Bank's income metric. Although the Bank claims that the MPI data complements its own findings, the latter initiative in fact yields a far higher percentage of poor people worldwide, while depicting the especially dire situation of the world's children. It should be remembered that to be MPI-poor requires 33 percent deprivation of basic life indicators; a somewhat less conservative threshold would have widened the gap between the MPI data and the World Bank's findings even further.

Measuring Global Hunger

Hunger is an important dimension of poverty, so we would do well to pay special attention to it. Has access to adequate nutrition risen or fallen globally in past decades? The UN's *Millennium Development Goals Report 2015* claims that global hunger is waning, but it does so based on questionable data from the UN's Food and Agriculture Organization (FAO). According to the UN report, the proportion of undernourished people in the developing countries has fallen by almost half since 1990, "from 23.3 percent in 1990–1992 to 12.9 percent in 2014–2016."

However, just as with the World Bank's poverty data, FAO hunger data and its methodology are extremely misleading. Everything points to the FAO having shifted goalposts to paint a rosier picture in time for the 2015 expiration of the Millennium Development Goals (MDGs). Jason Hickel has shown how the FAO changed its methods for gathering data on hunger in 2012, reversing its own earlier findings that world hunger had increased. Most notably, the new methodology involved "revised data on average population heights, which are used in turn to calculate the minimum dietary energy requirements" and reducing the calorie thresholds significantly downward at the end of the data collection period.[66] As a consequence, people needed *fewer calories* to be counted above the hunger threshold as the millennium progressed than they did in 1990, the reference year. As if this sleight-of-hand were not enough, the FAO kept revising upward its previous 1990 baseline figure of hungry people—the 786 million hungry people registered initially had become 980 million in later reports—thereby creating an illusion of progress.[67]

An additional problem is that the FAO's calculations on energy requirements are based on the claim that shorter people need fewer calories. Objectively this is true, but it confuses cause and effect. As Hickel notes, "shorter stature in a population is quite often a sign of undernourishment, so it makes little sense to conclude—as the FAO does—that as populations get shorter they require fewer calories. Indeed, in many cases, it is probable that the opposite is true."[68] Further, the FAO estimates the calories needed to avoid hunger based on a sedentary lifestyle, overlooking the physically exigent lifestyles of many people in the Third World.

If we measure hunger at the more accurate (and still conservative) level of calories required for normal activity, we see that 1.5

billion people are hungry, according to an annex in the FAO's 2012 report, which is twice as many as the UN would have us believe. If we measure hunger at the level of calories required for intense activity, the number of hungry is 2.5 billion. And the numbers are rising, not falling, even according to the new [FAO] methodology.[69]

There is an eerie parallel between the World Bank's metric for poverty and the FAO's metric for hunger: both use standards so removed from reality that they simply erase the problems they propose to measure. For the World Bank, the poverty threshold falls between one or two dollars daily, regardless of whether people can actually meet their fundamental needs with that sum. For the FAO, the hunger line is set at a minimum level of calories, regardless of real nutritional needs. Since the quality and content of these calories are not taken into account, people having serious vitamin or other nutrient deficiencies are not counted as undernourished.[70] Just as in Orwell's *1984*, the ministry of war is called the ministry of peace, so the impoverished in our world are not poor and the malnourished are not hungry!

Health Data

Without a doubt, the last thirty years have brought long overdue reductions in infant mortality, improvements in maternal health, and successful campaigns against AIDs, malaria, and other diseases. Reviewing UNICEF data, Steven Radelet celebrates this progress: "In 1990, 12.7 million children died before their fifth birthday from preventable causes; by 2013, the number was down to 6.3 million, and it continues to drop fast."[71] Turning to World Bank Development Indicators, he observes that the percentage of children dying under five in developing countries has declined from 22 percent in 1960 to just under 5 percent in 2013. As Radelet argues, much of this progress is attributable to expanded access to vaccines for the world's poor: "In 1980, only about 11% of children in developing countries were receiving the recommended three doses of the combined diphtheria, pertussis, and tetanus (DPT3) vaccine. Today more than 80% are fully vaccinated."[72] Likewise, the availability of basic oral rehydration therapy in the Third World has vastly reduced deaths from diarrhea, dropping from 5 million children every year in the early 1990s to 760,000 by 2013.[73]

How should we understand these successes, which are not negligible? True to his doctrine, Radelet credits neoliberal globalization for these advances. Yet the disturbing fact is that basic vaccines and health care could have been extended to the world's population long ago, saving millions of lives. All it would have taken is genuine aid from the rich nations, rather than bleeding peripheral countries dry through debt collection and other mechanisms of value transfer. The same ironies haunt the world's progress in reducing AIDS and malaria-related deaths. The progress is real, but it has been severely limited by patents that restrict the availability of medicines. According to the UN's *Millennium Development Goals Report 2015*:

> By June 2014, 13.6 million people living with HIV were receiving antiretroviral therapy (ART) globally, an immense increase from just 800,000 in 2003. ART averted 7.6 million deaths from AIDS between 1995 and 2013. . . . Over 6.2 million malaria deaths have been averted between 2000 and 2015, primarily of children under five years of age in sub-Saharan Africa. The global malaria incidence rate has fallen by an estimated 37 percent and the mortality rate by 58 percent.[74]

The Gates Foundation takes credit for combating the AIDs epidemic through its donations and work.[75] At the same time, Bill Gates and the Microsoft Corporation have consistently backed the World Trade Organization's Trade-Related Intellectual Property Rights treaty that has blocked African governments from buying generic AIDS, malaria, and tuberculosis medicines, thereby protecting the pharmaceutical industry.[76] Investigative journalist Greg Palast takes Gates to task on precisely this score:

Gates knows darn well that the "intellectual property rights" laws such as TRIPS—which keep him and Melinda richer than Saddam and the Mafia combined—are under attack by Nelson Mandela and front-line doctors trying to get cheap drugs to the 23 million Africans sick with the AIDS virus. Gates's brilliant and self-serving solution: he's spending an itsy-bitsy part of his monopoly profits (the $6 billion spent by Gates Foundation is less than 2% of his net worth) to buy some drugs for a fraction of the dying. The bully billionaire's "philanthropic" organization is currently working paw-in-claw with the big pharmaceutical companies in support of the blockade on cheap drug shipments.

Gates's game is given away by the fact that his Foundation has invested $200 million in the very drug companies stopping the shipment of low-cost AIDS drugs to Africa.

Gates says his plan is to reach one million people with medicine by the end of the decade. Another way to read it: he's locking in a trade system that will block the delivery of cheap medicine to over 20 million.[77]

In truth, instead of marveling at Gates's largess, we should ask how many lives could have been saved if corporations and unfair trade agreements had not hindered access to life-saving medicines (despite the protests of leaders such as Nelson Mandela). We should also ask why public health care systems throughout the so-called developing world are underfunded in the first place. The disastrous situation of health care in the periphery is the elephant in the room that explains both the recent Ebola epidemics and the fact that a single philanthropist such as Bill Gates could play such a huge role in shaping global health policies and services.

The recent overall improvement in basic health indicators should not obscure the fact that millions continue to die each year from preventable diseases, malnutrition, and poverty-related ailments. In its 2016 *State of the World's Children* report, UNICEF warns that "unless the world tackles inequity today . . . 69 million children under age 5 will die between 2016 and 2030."[78] This is nearly five million children who will die each year from preventable illnesses and poverty. In the words of Share the World's Resources, a research and information center:

According to calculations by Dr Gideon Polya based on figures from the UN Population Fund, over 17 million "avoidable deaths" occur every year as a consequence of life-threatening deprivation, mainly in low-income countries. The enormity of this statistic is supported by an array of figures periodically released by UN agencies, as well as earlier estimates made by STWR using World Health Organization data. As the term suggests, these preventable deaths occur simply because millions of people live in conditions of severe poverty and therefore cannot afford access to the essential goods and services that people in wealthier countries have long taken for granted—not even nutritious food or safe drinking water. The extent of this ongoing tragedy cannot be overstated when approximately 46,500 lives are wasted needlessly everyday—innocent men, women and children who might otherwise have contributed to the cultural and economic development of the world in unimaginable ways.[79]

Maternal mortality, or the death of women during pregnancy and childbirth, continues to be a major cause of avoidable deaths. Radelet notes that the number of mothers who died during childbirth *around the world* fell from 420 per 100,000 live births in 1990 to 238 in 2011.[80] This is, however, a *world* average, meaning that the rates in peripheral countries are much higher, while the gap between the Global North and South continues to widen. For example, if Sweden's maternal mortality rate is 4.6 and that of the United States is 16.7, Haiti's rate is a soaring 582.4.[81] An overall reduction of maternal mortality is indeed something to celebrate, but it should not whitewash an unjust world system that takes the lives of pregnant women in the Global South due to lack of health care, appropriate nutrition, and decent living conditions.

PRIMARY SCHOOL ENROLLMENT DATA

The UN's *Millennium Development Goals 2015* speaks of important increases in the number of children and especially girls enrolled in primary schools: "The primary school net enrolment rate in the developing regions has reached 91 percent in 2015, up from 83 percent in 2000. . . . The number of out-of-school children of primary school age worldwide has fallen by almost half, to an estimated 57 million in 2015, down from 100 million in 2000." Nevertheless, given that the UN misrepresents global poverty rates for the sake of political expedience, these claims should also be tested against experience and the findings of independent researchers. For example, the U.S.-installed Martelly regime in Haiti boasted of making primary education free and available to all. The World Bank dutifully echoed these claims:

> In 2011, President Martelly made education a cornerstone of his government program and launched the Universal, Free, and Compulsory Education Program. During the 2011–2012 school year, this program allowed more than one million children aged 6 to 12 to attend school free of charge.[82]

These "one million children" are surely among those swelling the ranks of enrolled students in the UN's 2015 *MDG Report*. The problem is—as Haitian educators, activists, and children know—the claim was false. It provided great PR for the Martelly regime and its Clinton Foundation backers, but it simply did not correspond with reality.[83]

In how many other cases did the World Bank and the UN, in their haste to relate uplifting stories, uncritically accept inflated statistics from corrupt regimes? Further, in how many cases are poor children technically enrolled in schools but effectively excluded from attending due to user fees (such as those that apply to books and uniforms) in increasingly privatized educational systems? Aside from these considerations, access to primary school does not necessarily mean that the children actually receive an education. According to recent

UNICEF data, 38 percent of the world's children leave primary school without learning how to read, write, and do simple arithmetic.[84]

THE STATUS OF GLOBAL SLUMS

The UN's 2015 *MDG Report* gives the impression that slums are slowly disappearing in the Third World. The proportion of those living in slums, it claims, fell from approximately 39.4 percent in 2000 to 29.7 percent in 2014. It is striking that this report chooses 2000 as the base year, instead of 1990, which was the usual one for UN Millennium Goals. If 1990 had been the starting point, a far more troubling picture would emerge. As the UN-HABITAT documented in the "main findings" of its 2003 report *Challenge of the Slums*:

> In 2001, 924 million people, or 31.6 percent of the world's urban population, lived in slums. The majority of them were in the developing regions, accounting for 43 percent of the urban population, in contrast to 6 percent in more developed regions. . . . *It is almost certain that slum dwellers increased substantially during the 1990s. It is further projected that in the next 30 years, the global number of slum dwellers will increase to about 2 billion, if no firm and concrete action is taken.* [Emphasis mine]

This 2003 report predicted that slum population would exceed one billion in just two years. If we fast forward to 2016, however, we find UN-Habitat telling a completely different story. A report from that year offers figures that happily coincide with the *MDG Report*:

> Recent estimates provided by UN-Habitat show that the proportion of the urban population living in slums in the developing countries decreased from 39.4 percent in 2000 to 29.7 percent in 2014. However, the absolute number stood at 881 million in 2014, compared with 791 million in the year 2000.[85]

What caused this about-face in UN-Habitat's reporting? Was there really a change in people's living situation or merely a change in methodology? In the case of poverty metrics, we have seen how the World Bank simply changed its standards to produce an upbeat 2015 *MDG Report*. Hence, we might legitimately wonder if a similar shifting of goalposts is behind the supposed decline in slum populations.

Taking the long view, we can see how the UN's 2015 *MDG Report* finds itself at odds with the well-established expansion of slums over the past fifty years. Millions of peasants in the Global South have been violently displaced from their lands in recent decades. The causes include the pressure from corporate competition unleashed by U.S.-imposed "free trade" policies; growing agribusiness control over seeds and the food system; and land grabs by mining and farming corporations.[86] Philip McMichael, an expert on agrarian issues at Cornell University, explains this process:

> Peasant dispossession intensified with the deepening of colonial mechanisms of primitive accumulation [e.g., land grabs] by post-colonial states. From 1950 to 1997, the world's rural population decreased by some 25%, and now 63% of the world's urban population dwells in, and on the margins of, sprawling cities of the Global South.[87]

This huge, global demographic shift has given rise to what Mike Davis calls the "planet of slums." Shantytowns, populated by an ever-growing "reserve army of the unemployed," have proliferated throughout urban centers from Port-au-Prince to Jakarta.

Davis's classic study on the subject, published in 2006, found that slum dwellers constitute almost 80 percent of urbanites in the least-developed countries and a third of the global population in cities.[88] He warned that the problem of slums was far worse than UN statistics depict, due in part to an overly restrictive definition of slums. In Mexico, Davis contrasted the UN's "counter-experiential finding" that only 19.6 percent live in slums with the fact that local experts believe that almost two-thirds of Mexicans dwell in irregular housing or older tenements.[89]

It is hardly accidental that the UN's 2015 *MDG Report* ignores this violent, historical process of displacement. Most of capitalism's apologists consider displacement to be part and parcel of progress and development. The eviction and migration of peasants and indigenous peoples into urban slums accounts for much of the alleged reduction of extreme poverty in recent years. In urban contexts they may now be living in grinding poverty, having left behind a traditional world that provided for many basic needs outside of a market economy. Yet if they scrape together a measly $1.90 or more per day, they have crossed the poverty threshold. As economist Michael Yates put it:

> The World Bank has been instrumental in promoting large-scale export agriculture in poor countries. Many persons living below the World Bank poverty level are subsistence peasants operating outside the money economy. Their economic well-being is often greater than a dollar a day would indicate. As they are in effect dispossessed by Bank-promoted agriculture and move into urban areas, their money income may exceed the World Bank poverty level, but, in fact, they are considerably worse off than they were in the countryside.[90]

The real-life costs of abandoning a sustainable rural economy do not figure in World Bank statistics. However, Gary Leech gives a good picture of what is really at stake in an article titled "Distorting Poverty to Promote Capitalism," which is worth quoting at length:

> In most countries the cost of living in urban areas is significantly higher than in rural regions, particularly with regard to food and housing. So while many of these new urban residents earn a higher income by rummaging through municipal garbage dumps in search of any item of value they can sell as illegal street vendors, this income is often insufficient to meet their basic food needs and other increased costs of living such as housing, utilities and transportation. Consequently, despite now

earning more than $1.25 a day, or even surpassing the poverty level income of $2.00 a day, many migrants who have moved to urban areas face even greater economic insecurity than they did in the countryside.

This economic (and poverty) reality is evident in a 2009 United Nations report which states, "Despite higher rates of poverty in rural areas, rural food insecurity is not necessarily higher than that in the cities. In fact . . . in 12 of 18 selected low-income developing countries, the incidence of food insecurity (as measured by food-energy deficiency) in urban areas is the same or higher than in the countryside, even though urban areas on average have higher incomes."

One of the problems is the fact that the limited financial resources of the urban poor also have to cover the higher urban costs of housing, utilities and transportation among other things. Therefore, as the UN report notes, "Food security in the cities thus depends to a large extent on individual household circumstances as the household operates within this purchasing environment. The question becomes whether the relatively higher income compared to rural dwellers can compensate for what may be higher food prices and demands to spend remaining income on other needs, as well as the much lower capacity to buffer food price shocks by actually growing or raising the food the family need."

Not only do many migrants to urban areas face increased economic insecurity despite achieving higher income levels, but they are also forced to endure the skyrocketing levels of violent crime that is the brutal reality of daily life in many cities in the Global South. Many also struggle to cope with the disintegration of the social networks and cultural practices prevalent in their rural communities, social and cultural practices often directly linked to nature and the land.[91]

If migration from rural areas results in a form of "progress" that is synonymous with urban misery, we might try to attack the problem from a different angle.[92] We could instead address what makes life unbearable for peasants worldwide. This is precisely the aim of the social movement Via Campesina, which tries to secure government support for farmers and more equitable land ownership. Trying to make a decent, sustainable life for small farmers, however, does not count as "good news" for the UN or the World Bank.

DRINKING WATER AND SANITATION

To complete its upbeat narrative the UN's *MDG Report 2015* asserts that there have been dramatic improvements in access to drinking water and improved sanitation for populations in the Global South:

> Of the 2.6 billion people who have gained access to improved drinking water since 1990, 1.9 billion gained access to piped drinking water on premises. Over half of the global population (58 percent) now enjoys this higher level of service.... Worldwide, 2.1 billion people have gained access to improved sanitation. The proportion of people practicing open defecation has fallen almost by half since 1990.

Two simple points should be made here. First, the whole world could have had access to decent plumbing, water, and sanitation long ago. All it would have taken is for the United States and other OECD countries to shell out meager funds for infrastructure development. This is money that is owed to the peoples of the Global South, as reparations for the crimes of colonialism and slavery. Second, the words *access* and *improved* call for careful scrutiny. Since so many basic utilities, including water, are being privatized in poor countries, *access* is often mediated by user fees that exclude the poor. Technically, the poor in Port-au-Prince may have "access to improved drinking water," but can they afford it? The same goes for electricity. Leaving aside these questions, the UN report shows that, well into the twenty-first century, nearly half of the world's population is without drinking water in their homes.

Conclusion to Part One

The UN, the World Bank, and the chorus of neoliberal ideologues tell us a story that is well suited to their class interests. Global capitalism is drawing an ever-larger number of people out of poverty, hunger, and disease. Their metrics and data, as we have seen, are deeply problematic. If any reasonable measure of poverty is used, such as the UNCTAD threshold of five dollars a day, it is clear that the number of people in the world living in poverty has increased dramatically since 1990. While this has occurred, global inequality has increased, contributing to a widening divergence between the core and peripheral countries, rather than the "convergence" celebrated by champions of global capitalism.

There is, however, one method of measuring global inequality that demonstrates convergence. This method involves 1) determining the per capita income of each country (total income divided by population); 2) giving countries with larger populations more weight when determining the inequality ratio, or Gini coefficient, between rich and poor countries. Using this method, former World Bank economist Branko Milanovic demonstrates that since 1990 there has been an impressive convergence between poor and rich countries, which is due exclusively to the growth in the per capita incomes of China and India. Michael Yates summarizes these findings:

After 1990, there is a sharp convergence. While most poor countries are not converging, the two largest ones, China and India, are. Incomes for hundreds of millions of Chinese and Indians have risen dramatically, and because these nations have a combined population of 2.7 billion—37.5 percent of the world's population—they count for much more than most nations in terms of national income. They alone account for the convergence. . . . If we excluded them, there would be no convergence between rich and poor places.[93]

It should be kept in mind that the average income in China and India is buoyed up by the growing fraction of billionaires in those countries, which raises average per capita income without significantly improving the conditions of the majority. In 2016, the BBC reported that China had 594 billionaires, a greater number than the United States.[94] According to *Forbes* magazine the 100 richest people in India were all billionaires, with petroleum magnate Mukesh Ambani having a net worth of $22.7 billion.[95]

Moreover, as Jason Hickel points out, the arguments for global convergence are based upon the *relative* rate at which per capita incomes are growing:

So if the [per capita] incomes of poor countries [like India and China] increase at a rate slightly faster than the incomes of rich ones, the Gini index shows declining inequality even if the absolute gap between them has grown. Here is an example. If a poor country's income goes up from $5,000 to $5,500 (a 10% increase), and a rich country's income goes up from $50,000 to $54,500 (a 9% increase), the Gini index shows *decreasing* inequality because the income of the poor country is growing faster than that of the rich country, even though the gap between them has *grown* by $4,000.[96]

If we look at the actual gap between per capita incomes of rich and poor countries, instead of the *relative growth* of average incomes, the data overwhelmingly indicates that global inequality has been rising.

> Using data from the Maddison Project, we see that in 1960, at the end of colonialism, people living in the world's richest country were 33 times richer than people living in the poorest country. That's quite a substantial gap. But then by 2000, after neoliberal globalization had run its course, they were a shocking 134 times richer. And that's not counting extreme outliers, like small oil-rich kingdoms in the Middle East or tiny offshore tax havens. This isn't convergence. To quote Lant Pritchett, it's divergence, big time.
>
> If we look at it in absolute terms, it's just as bad. From 1960 to today, based on the data from the Maddison Project, the absolute gap between the average incomes of people in the richest and poorest countries has grown by 135%.
>
> Of course, this metric overstates inequality by focusing on countries at either extreme. We can correct for this by looking at regional differences. The best way to do this is to measure the gap, in real terms, between the GDP per capita of the world's dominant power (the United States) and that of various regions of the Global South. Using World Bank figures, we see that since 1960 the gap for Latin America has grown by 206%, the gap for sub-Saharan Africa has grown by 207%, and the gap for South Asia has grown by 196%. In other words, the global inequality gap has roughly tripled in size.[97]

This is the context in which Oxfam issued its scathing 2016 report on global inequality, showing how economic growth has failed to benefit the majority:

> The gap between rich and poor is reaching new extremes. Credit Suisse recently revealed that the richest 1% have now accumulated more wealth than the rest of the world put together. This occurred a year earlier than Oxfam's much publicized prediction

ahead of last year's World Economic Forum. Meanwhile, the wealth owned by the bottom half of humanity has fallen by a trillion dollars in the past five years. This is just the latest evidence that today we live in a world with levels of inequality we may not have seen for over a century.[98]

Four years have gone by since the MDGs 2015 deadline, and the world is clearly becoming more unequal, with a majority of humanity still living in poverty. The World Bank and most of the UN establishment continue to write neoliberal prescriptions, updated with fashionable catchphrases like "shared prosperity" and "sustainability," all the while obfuscating the scale and scope of the human and environmental holocaust. Neoliberal cheerleaders, who applaud as the capitalist locomotive approaches the precipice, are indeed irritating and dangerous. Yet to put the brakes on this tragedy, we will need more than just protests against neoliberalism and its formulas. Instead, it is imperative to understand that neoliberalism is itself a manifestation of imperialism. This is understood by peoples and movements that have lived under imperialism's boot, but leftists in the rich countries often delude themselves into thinking that the imperialist system, which provides for their comfortable lives, will not have to be brought down. It was against imperialism that our friend mentioned in the introduction, the Haitian journalist, struggled consciously and bravely, before poverty and disease killed him. The second part of this book will be devoted to explaining the imperialist world system that took his life and the lives of so many others.

PART TWO

GOING
BEYOND
STATISTICS
TO THE
DYNAMICS
OF
IMPERIALISM

Cobalt miners in the Congo

3. Causes and Consequences of the Neoliberal Phase of Imperialism

Statistics about poverty show us that there is a problem, even a crisis, but they do not tell us why. Beyond the statistics, it is important to understand the forces behind the expansion of global poverty and inequality. This takes us away from the amorphous concept of globalization to an analysis of imperialism as it has evolved since the Second World War.

Neoliberalism is a phase of imperialism. It is a particular expression of capitalist globalization that took shape in the early 1970s and spread across the world from the late 1970s to the present. Key neoliberal policies include removing controls and barriers to cross-border trade and investment, especially by transnational corporations; promoting "free trade" agreements; reducing taxes on capital and the wealthy; deregulating finance capital domestically and internationally; and cutting public services and welfare programs.

The U.S. government has played a central role in imposing the neoliberal agenda on the global economy since the Reagan administration and no matter whether the government was controlled by Republicans or Democrats. To do so, it has worked hand-in-hand with the multilateral financial institutions it dominates, such as the World Bank and the International Monetary Fund. These institutions have been especially important in reshaping Third World countries in a neoliberal manner through the imposition of structural adjustment packages. In 1995, the General Agreement on Tariffs and Trade (GATT) morphed into the World Trade Organization (WTO), further consolidating neoliberalism as the operating logic of the global economy. There is an ample bibliography of critical writings on neoliberalism that can be consulted by those interested in further reading.[99]

Neoliberal policies, because they deregulate capital, freeing it from institutional constraints, have been extremely destructive to people and the environment. For this reason, the neoliberal project should be adamantly opposed, and many social movements, scholars, and policymakers have done so. It should be kept in view, however, that neoliberalism is a variant of global capitalism, which emerged following the profit squeeze and stagnation of the 1970s. In other words, neoliberalism is a symptom of a bigger problem. We must examine the whole system and the forces that move it. Global capitalism, of which neoliberalism is an extension, cannot be understood outside of the context of an imperialist world system. It was imperialism, more than any other factor, that established capitalism as a global system, and capitalism-made-global has in turn invigorated and transformed imperialism. This means that to struggle against neoliberalism without confronting global capitalism, or to struggle against capitalism without confronting twenty-first century imperialism, is to tilt at windmills.

Imperialism has various guises, but all involve a "taking" of resources, including labor, of one country by another. This taking has always been done by the rich capitalist nations, subordinating the people in the nations comprising what we today call the Global South. Wealth and income in the form of surplus value always flows from Global South to Global North. Through this process, the imperialist countries develop by "underdeveloping" the dominated countries. It is capitalism that generates imperialism and neoliberalism. In the beginning, it was the massive enslavement of Africans and the rise of European colonialism—predicated upon mass dispossession and genocide of indigenous populations—that fueled capitalist development and generated the key wealth of the leading capitalist powers, including the United States.

Later, with capitalism firmly established as the dominant world system, competition between the leading capitalist powers and their corporations for global raw materials and markets intensified. This dynamic of inter-imperialist competition, together with the emerging prominence of finance capital, inspired Lenin to write his *Imperialism: The Highest Stage of Capitalism*, in 1917. It was during this stage of capitalism that an extreme polarization of the world took place. On the one hand, the imperialist powers—primarily the United States, Western Europe, and, to a lesser extent, Japan—emerged to form what is variously known as the developed or core countries (those belonging to the First World or Global North). Meanwhile, the countries they dominated in Asia, Africa, Latin America, and the Middle East became the underdeveloped or peripheral countries (those belonging to the Third World or Global South). The core countries used the raw materials and minerals plundered from colonies and neo-colonies as inputs to their industries, which in turn sold their products in core-country markets and also in markets composed of the privileged classes in the periphery. In doing so, the core countries expropriated the land and raw materials of the periphery, allowing them to accumulate vast amounts of surplus value by exploiting the labor of colonized workers and peasants. This exploitation created a huge gap between the value of labor power in the periphery and the core, giving rise to *unequal exchange*: the compressed value of the raw materials from the periphery versus the inflated value of the manufactured products from the core.[100]

After the Second World War, the United States replaced Britain as the leading imperialist power, presiding over a new global economic order in which U.S. corporations increasingly penetrated the markets in the periphery once monopolized by European corporations. The Bretton Woods Conference of 1944 established the U.S. dollar as the world's reserve currency, against which other currencies would be pegged in fixed ratios, with the dollar itself pegged to gold. The United States also came to dominate the newly formed World Bank and International Monetary Fund. Planning documents of the U.S. State Department and the Council on Foreign Relations reveal a concerted, conscious effort to maintain and expand the U.S. empire.[101] The United States used both the General Agreement on Tariffs and Trade (GATT) and selective "free trade" policies, together with the Marshall Plan, to strengthen its hegemonic position in the global economy.

In the late 1940s and 1950s a wave of independence movements gained momentum and began to come to power in Third World countries. India broke with the British Empire to became independent in 1947, and Ghana did so in 1957. These movements represented major obstacles to the global projection of U.S. imperialism. Their leaders ranged from relatively orthodox Marxists such as Kwame Nkrumah in Ghana and Mao Zedong in China to progressive nationalists like Patrice Lumumba in Congo, Jacobo Arbenz in Guatemala, and Mohammad Mossaddeq in Iran.

Whether in government or struggling for power, these national liberation movements sought to redistribute wealth and power to the people. They typically pursued land reform and the selective nationalization of key resources (such as oil in Iran), with a view to achieving economic justice and overcoming underdevelopment. Such measures were anathema to the U.S. government insofar as they threatened existing and future projects of its corporations. For example, the United Fruit Company perceived Arbenz's progressive government in Guatemala as a threat. Often alleging the specter of communism, the U.S. government set out to destroy these movements and progressive governments. The result was a seemingly unending series of forced regime changes and interventions: the United States overthrew Mossaddeq and Arbenz; facilitated the assassination of Lumumba; blocked nationwide elections in Vietnam, before invading the south of that country; organized the Bay of Pigs invasion of Cuba; supported Suharto's bloodbath in Indonesia; and invaded the Dominican

Republic.[102] This systematic repression of Third World peoples was the background for Dr. Martin Luther King, Jr.'s 1967 speech against the Vietnam War, in which he referred to the U.S. government as the "greatest purveyor of violence in the world."

By the early 1970s, the United States had established an extensive network of client dictatorships in the Global South to guarantee "friendly investment climates" for its corporations. That worldwide network, together with a system of military bases of similar extension, constituted the largest empire in human history. Though the countries it included were for the most part nominally independent, they were ruled by brutal and corrupt puppet regimes sustained by U.S. military aid, training, and economic support (along with support by the World Bank, itself controlled by the United States).[103] Whenever an independent progressive leader came to power, as was the case with Salvador Allende in Chile in 1970, the World Bank and other U.S.-led agencies withdrew their support, while the CIA did the dirty work to depose him. Western European countries and Japan were junior partners in this imperial network, organized through such alliances as NATO, the OECD, and the Trilateral Commission. Pretending to defend the "Free World" from "communism" and "Soviet aggression," these alliances actually facilitated the ongoing control and plunder of the periphery.

In 1965, Ghanaian independence leader Kwame Nkrumah wrote the book *Neo-Colonialism: The Last Stage of Imperialism*, in which he analyzed this network of nominally independent but still subordinated states as a form of neocolonialism. As the book's title indicates, Nkrumah considered neocolonialism to be a phase of imperialism. That phase continues to this day, although many Third World dictatorships have given way to superficial or fraudulent "democracies" while real power remains in the hands of a comprador bourgeoisie and their imperialist governments and corporate backers. Within this continuity, however, there have been some important changes. Beginning in the early 1970s, U.S.-led global capitalism restructured itself to respond to three new challenges: 1) the decline of the dollar; 2) the falling rate of corporate profit in the core countries and a trend toward economic stagnation; and 3) the Third World "debt crisis." Faced with these challenges, U.S. corporate and government leaders did not remain passive. Instead, they leveraged obstacles into opportunities. The result was what is commonly called neoliberalism. The story of these challenges and how the establishment's responses to them worked to deepen world poverty is told in the following sections.

THE DECLINE OF THE DOLLAR

In the 1960s, the Japanese and West German economies recovered, but the U.S. share of the global economy began to modestly decline, in part due to massive spending on the Vietnam War. Some countries in the OECD began to sense that the dollar was overvalued. For this reason, Switzerland and France moved to redeem millions of their dollars for gold, raising the danger of a run on the dollar (which was a serious concern, given that the U.S. government did not have enough gold reserves to redeem all dollars held by foreign central banks). In early 1971, Germany left the Bretton Woods system, allowing the deutsche mark to float in relation to the dollar. These events were the background for the famous "Nixon shock" of August 15, 1971. Claiming that his aim was to protect the dollar from "attacks of international money speculators," Nixon announced that greenbacks would no longer be backed by gold, effectively ending the Bretton Woods system of fixed exchange rates.[104]

Now that the dollar had lost its backing in gold, what would protect its value, both nationally and internationally? Would it continue to be the international reserve currency? In fact, the dollar did depreciate considerably after Nixon's decision. Nevertheless, in 1973 the Organization of Petroleum Exporting Countries announced an oil embargo. The aim was ostensibly to punish the West for supporting Israel in the Yom Kippur War, but the embargo was surely also intended to boost oil prices, which had not risen proportionally with other major commodities. It proved effective. By 1974, the price of oil had quadrupled.

In these years, Henry Kissinger and other members of the Nixon administration consolidated a "special relationship" with the Saudi Arabian monarchy that would prove determinative in future decades. The deal struck was that Saudi Arabia would sell oil for dollars and then use part of the excess dollars, the so-called petrodollars, to purchase U.S. Treasury bonds, thereby boosting the value of the dollar and enabling the U.S. government to easily borrow money. The U.S.-Saudi Arabian Joint Commission on Economic Cooperation, founded in June 1975, was the formal recognition of this deal.[105] In exchange for Saudi cooperation, the U.S. government provided the monarchy with technology (especially weapons) and infrastructure investment. Historian Greg Grandin argues that Kissinger's deal with the Saudis was a replay of the relationship forged earlier with the Shah of Iran. By 1975, the United States had "more than a trillion dollars' worth of military agreements with Riyadh."[106] The United States got the Saudis to pressure other OPEC countries to standardize the sale of oil in dollars. In effect, oil replaced gold as the dollar's backing in the emerging international system.

It is still debated whether the Nixon administration was complicit in the oil crisis, helping to engineer it to weaken economic competition from Japan and Germany. What is undeniable, however, is that the administration successfully leveraged the crisis into an opportunity to solidify the dollar as the world's reserve currency for oil.[107] At the same time, by terminating the Bretton Woods system of fixed exchange rates, Nixon paved the way for financial deregulation and international speculation on currencies: key pillars of the neoliberal world order that reigns today.

THE DECLINING RATE OF PROFIT

The second challenge facing U.S. capitalism in the early 1970s was the declining rate of corporate profit and a trend toward economic stagnation. In response, some corporations began outsourcing the production of textiles and basic electronics to low-wage countries, establishing export platforms that would later become widespread.

Martin Hart-Landsberg's excellent study, *The Internationalization of Production*, explains this process:

> Parts and components were sent to these export platforms; low-wage Third World workers performed operations on them; and the intermediate products were shipped back to the United States for final assembly and sale. Although these foreign operations were limited to relatively simple labor-intensive tasks, their activities were integral to home-country operations and profitability.[108]

Despite this move, the U.S. trade deficit with Japan and Germany continued to grow. In response, the U.S. government negotiated the 1985 Plaza Accord, in which the Japanese and German governments agreed to a significant revaluation of their currencies, thereby undercutting the competitiveness of their exports to the U.S. market. Japanese corporations responded by outsourcing production to the ASEAN-3 countries (Indonesia, Malaysia, and Thailand), establishing export platforms there to benefit from lower wages. South Korea, Taiwan, Hong Kong, and Singapore—the Asian Tigers—followed Japan's lead by also outsourcing production to the ASEAN-3. Though highly dependent upon Japanese investments and sales, the Asian Tigers also developed powerful corporations that competed with Japan for exports to the U.S. market.

Foreign direct investment (FDI) grew dramatically in the 1980s. "Between 1983 and 1989," Hart-Landsberg explains, "world FDI outflows grew at a compound annual rate of 28.9%, compared with a compound annual growth rate of 9.4% of world exports and 7.8% for world gross domestic product."[109] Outsourcing was key to this boom in FDI, and it shifted from simple products to more sophisticated manufactures such as automobiles, televisions, computers, semiconductors, and pharmaceuticals. Yet the extent of outsourcing is far larger than what is achieved through FDI; outsourcing is also now accomplished through "arm's-length" contracting and other mechanisms that establish global relations of production through what appear to be market exchanges.[110]

In a vital reshaping of U.S. imperialism, corporations were now relocating industrial production to the periphery, often to Export Processing Zones (EPZs). These are sometimes called "free zones," and in fact provide an almost complete freedom to capital. Corporations send raw materials and intermediate goods into the zones, where environmental and labor regulations are minimal, to make products for (re)export. This reconfiguration of global capitalism has had huge consequences, with developing countries' share of the world's industrial employment growing rapidly (it passed from 52 percent in 1980 to 83 percent by 2012).[111] China's shift to capitalism and its transformation into a global platform for export-oriented production has helped accelerate this tendency. John Smith, who considers outsourcing and arm's-length contracts as central to the functioning of imperialism, describes this shift of manufacturing to the periphery:

EPZs have experienced accelerating growth—the numbers employed in them nearly tripled between 1997 and 2006, the latest year for which there are statistics, when 63 million workers were employed in EPZs located in 132 countries…. EPZs were responsible for 75% or more of export earnings in Kenya, Malaysia, Madagascar, Vietnam, Dominican Republic, and Bangladesh, while Philippines, Mexico, Haiti, and Morocco earned 50% to 60% of exports from their EPZs. The ILO [International Labor Organisation] Employment in EPZs database reports that Asia's 900+ zones employed 53 million workers, 40 million of them in China and 3.25 million in Bangladesh.[112]

EPZs are paradises for capital, but for labor they are the very opposite. The 1996 documentary *Mickey Mouse Goes to Haiti: Walt Disney and the Science of Exploitation*, offers a window on the grueling working and living conditions of the men, women, and children who labor in EPZs across the globe. What one sees is a truly dire situation. Yet, since the Haitian workers in the film were earning approximately $2.40 per day making garments for Disney, they cleared the World Bank's poverty line by a long shot. In the eyes of the World Bank, they were dangerously close to being "middle class," despite malnutrition and living in overcrowded slums with no access to plumbing or consistent electricity, to say nothing of health care or decent education. There is no shortage of statistics showing the importance of this global restructuring of production. For example, John Smith records how developing countries' "share of imperialist nations' manufactured imports [has] rocketed since 1980, more than tripling their share of a cake that itself quadrupled in the subsequent three decades."[113] This is a massive change in the world's productive apparatus and it goes far beyond what FDI flows indicate. The data show that after 2010, FDI began to flow principally to developing countries.[114] Indeed, investment in the periphery is of greater importance than it appears on paper because of the extremely high rate of profit that such investment yields and because it is actually productive investment, whereas FDI between core countries is exaggerated by nonproductive investments in finance, mergers and acquisitions, and is sometimes even a disguised version of investment in the periphery.[115]

Additionally, much of what the Third World produces for core markets, whether in EPZs or other settings, occurs outside of FDI. Instead, it is done through "arm's-length contracting" between a transnational corporation in an imperialist country and a separate firm in a low-wage country. Arm's-length contracting has become a preferred method of exploitation, both because it absolves the core countries' corporations of liability for what occurs in the foreign production center and because it pressures contractors to compete with one another to lower unit production costs. Global labor arbitrage of this kind allows Apple to reap extremely high profits from its smartphones. The Taiwanese company Foxconn first produces the iPhone, which is then purchased by Apple and sold primarily in core-country markets. These networks of cross-border production, dominated by core country corporations and facilitated by arm's-length contracting, are known as *global value chains* (GVCs).

Linking peripheral and core economies, GVCs are the mechanism par excellence of today's imperialism. Their influence is huge. According to the United Nations Conference on Trade and

Development (UNCTAD) 2013 *World Investment Report,* global chains controlled by transnational corporations account for about 80 percent of global trade.[116] The same report confirms that

> about 60 percent of global trade, which today amounts to more than $20 trillion, consists of trade in intermediate goods and services that are incorporated at various stages in the production process of goods and services for final consumption. The fragmentation of production processes and the international dispersion of tasks and activities within them have led to the emergence of borderless production systems.[117]

In the core countries' economies, GVC-related trade is now central. For the United States, about two-thirds of imports and exports involve the GVCs of transnational corporations. For Japan, the figure is even higher, closer to 85 percent.[118]

China, like the Asian Tigers, plays an intermediate, sub-imperialist role in this system. Evidently, China produces massively for export, as part of a peripheral link in value chains controlled by the core countries' transnational corporations (TNCs). According to the Asian Development Bank, China functions as "an assembly hub for final products in Asian production networks" that are then exported to core-country markets.[119] The core countries' TNCs maintain tight control over much of China's economy, which mostly contributes cheap labor, with Chinese workers experiencing brutal exploitation and job insecurity, despite World Bank claims that China has lifted nearly a billion out of poverty. Not only do transnational corporations produce most of China's high-technology exports (85 percent) but the share produced by wholly foreign-owned transnationals appears to be growing.[120]

This, however, is only half the picture, for Chinese corporations also show important signs of independence. In 2016, Forbes reported that 249 of the world's biggest corporations are now based in China, more than the number in Germany or Japan and only surpassed by the United States.[121] While these Chinese corporations are undoubtedly

sometimes integrated, through GVCs, with their core-country counterparts, they are also potential rivals. In effect, the current trend is
for Chinese corporations to participate in imperialism. In keeping
with this imperialist profile, China is becoming a major consumer of
resources and raw materials from Latin America and Africa, which it
transforms into final goods for markets in the Global North:

> While Latin America and sub-Saharan nations have long spe-
> cialized in the export of primary commodities, developing Asia,
> especially China, has now replaced core capitalist countries as
> their main export market. China has surpassed the United States
> as the world's largest consumer of major metals and agricultural
> commodities. In 2011, it consumed 20% of all nonrenewable
> energy sources, 23% of major agricultural crops, and 40% of
> base metals. . . . China is pouring billions of dollars into Latin
> American investments to expand the region's capacity to pro-
> duce key primary products it currently buys from the region,
> primarily iron, copper, soy, and petroleum. At the same time,
> its manufactures undermine the region's own efforts at indus-
> trialization. Kevin P. Gallagher, a specialist in China-Latin
> American economic relations, estimated that in 2009, 92% of
> Latin American and Caribbean manufacturing exports were
> under direct or partial threat from Chinese exports. [122]

In effect, growing Chinese demand is inducing a destructive process of deindustrialization in Latin America and sub-Saharan African
countries, where already limited manufacturing sectors are giving
way to raw material exports, services, and resource extraction.

The relationship between Chinese capitalism and U.S. imperialism is contradictory. On the one hand, the United States has provided
the consumer market, much of the foreign investment and arm's
length contracts, as well as the international institutions such as the
World Trade Organization that have all been indispensable to the
capitalist transformation of China. On the other hand, the Chinese
are not passive partners in this process. Just as the initiative for the

transformation came from Deng Xiaoping and forces within China, there are now some sectors within the Chinese capitalist class and state apparatus that are pursuing their own imperialist agendas. In this sense, military budgets are revealing. By 2012, the United States was spending $682.5 billion on its military, approximately 40 percent of the world total. Yet the country coming into second place was China, spending $166.1 billion on its military. Though it amounted to only 9.5 percent of the world's total military expenditures, China's spending in this area has almost tripled over the past decade.[123]

The BRICS power bloc, composed of Brazil, Russia, India, China, and South Africa, the so-called emerging countries of the semi-periphery, also shows a contradictory development that defies simple characterizations. On the one hand, the BRICS cannot be reduced to a mere extension of U.S. imperialism (an analysis reminiscent of the erroneous "ultra-imperialist" standpoint that reduces imperialism to a single homogenous network). On the other hand, neither does the BRICS group represent an independent progressive challenge or a "great surge" of the South. The reality is more dialectical. As with China, much of the GDP growth of the BRICS is fueled directly or indirectly by U.S. corporations through foreign direct investment, arm's length contracts, and loans. Moreover, the BRICS countries participate in international institutions that are key to maintaining the imperialist world order. For example, a Brazilian now directs the World Trade Organization, aggressively pursuing "free trade," while Chinese and Indian economists play central roles in the World Bank and the IMF.[124]

Undoubtedly, the BRICS countries have staked out positions and built trade relationships that clash with U.S. and core-country dominance. One important area of contention is resistance to the dollar as the international currency. For example, in 2014 Russia agreed to supply gas to China using local currencies, not the U.S. dollar, thereby partially reducing Russia's dependence on sales to the European market.[125] Russia and India have also resisted core country demands to restrict intellectual property rights. Finally, the BRICS countries have worked to create alternative financial institutions.

These include the New Development Bank created in 2014 and China's Asian Infrastructure Bank, founded in 2016 and sometimes viewed as a rival to the World Bank.[126] Washington found the former initiative to be sufficiently neoliberal as to complement its objectives, but, along with Japan, it boycotted the latter project.[127] In summary, the BRICS power bloc operates as an intermediate or semi-peripheral force in the imperialist system, even if it sometimes conflicts with U.S. neocolonialism and core country interests. It is against this backdrop that NATO decided to expand its military encirclement around Russia and launched the U.S. "Pacific Pivot" to further militarize that region.

In essence, the old imperialist system—in which the core countries extracted raw materials, minerals, and primary commodities from the periphery and then manufactured them into final products within the core country itself—has given way to a new, more complex system. Now, it is the "emerging" countries like China that do the manufacturing, and their people must bear the full brunt of exploitation and the externalities of production. The new system not only successfully displaces the damage of extraction and pillage to the periphery (as in the earlier system), but it also maintains the exploitation of labor at arm's length from the core country.[128] Furthermore, despite the rise of the BRICS and evidence of some inter-imperialist contradictions, the ultimate destination of most products and profits in this system is still, primarily, the core countries and especially the United States. UNCTAD's 2013 Trade and Development Report explains:

> United States personal consumption, amounting to about $10 trillion, represented around 70 percent of that country's GDP and about 16 percent of global GDP; consumer spending also accounted for over 70 percent of United States GDP growth during the period 2000–2007. Most importantly, imports of consumer goods, including automobiles, accounted for about 85 percent of the increase in the United States' non-energy trade deficit between 1997 and 2007. Over the same period, imports of non-food consumer goods, excluding automobiles, increased

by about 150 percent, boosting aggregate demand in the rest of the world by almost $300 billion in absolute terms.[129]

The United States remains, then, the world's center of consumption, what Yanis Varoufakis calls the "Global Minotaur" because of its role as a sink for global surpluses (similar to the sacrificial tributes fed to the mythical Minotaur).[130] Not surprisingly, the U.S. economy has the world's greatest trade deficit, buying far more from foreign countries than it exports to the world—except for military equipment, including massive amounts of weapons. U.S. trade deficits, buttressed by the artificially strong dollar, have sustained the world's export-led growth. According to an UNCTAD report, "In 2006, the U.S. accounted for approximately half of the world's aggregate current account deficits, while China accounted for one-fourth of the world's aggregate current account surpluses."[131] The artificial strength of the dollar, a result of its function as the world's reserve currency and its privileged status in oil markets, allows the United States to run a huge trade deficit without experiencing a painful devaluation of its currency. A key support of the dollar is the special understanding the United States has with key trading partners, including Saudi Arabia and other oil producers, to the effect that they will recycle much of their economic surplus back to the United States by purchasing Treasury bonds. That circuit enables the United States to accrue national debt without facing the austerity measures that would be imposed on a peripheral economy if it were to run so high a deficit. Michele Brand and Remy Herrera describe this arrangement:

> The dollar is vastly overvalued in relation to the real U.S. economy, which consumes much more than it produces and makes up the difference with debt. The combined deficits of the federal budget and the current account come to around one trillion dollars per year. No other country could live so much above its means with impunity. Without this international demand for dollars, the dollar would "correct," and U.S. hegemony would eventually, inevitably, come to an end.[132]

This system is deeply twisted and polarizing. The suppression of wages in countries like China and Bangladesh and the extractive plunder of Congo and other countries underwrites the obscene levels of consumption in the Global North. Although many shoppers in the rich nations are working class, their access to cheap goods produced in super-exploitative conditions can often override class conscious- ness. Sadly, for many of these consumers the premiere of a novel video game or the new season of a television series seems more worthy of attention than the latest imperialist intervention. As the IMF noted in its *World Economic Outlook 2007* report, "Although the labor share [of GDP] went down, globalization of labor as manifested in cheaper imports in advanced [core] economies has increased the 'size of the pie' to be shared among all citizens, resulting in a net gain in total workers' compensation in real terms."[133]

Undoubtedly, neoliberalism and the extension of production chains across the globe have yielded favorable results for major corporations. In 2013, U.S. corporations were logging record profits, even though such profits were not usually reinvested in domestic production and the secular, long-term trend toward stagnation continues.[134] Hence, the neoliberal form of capitalism is not a harmonious "global village" but rather a deeper form of U.S. imperialism.[135] The radical deregula- tion of international currency and financial markets, together with the growth of cross-border trade and investments, has widened the gap between rich and poor countries. The Global South is more chained than ever to imperialist structures of production and trade, with consumption patterns now disproportionately dictated by core- country corporations. Although internal markets may be expanding somewhat in the Global South, this does not fundamentally alter the imperialist nature of the global economy. An UNCTAD report explains the limited impact of South-South trade:

A disaggregation of developing countries' total exports by major product categories indicates little change in the two main characteristics of South-South trade, namely its narrow concen- tration in Asia, related to these countries' strong involvement in international production networks, with developed countries as final destination markets, and the major role of primary commodities in the expansion of South-South trade over the past two decades. . . . Taken together, there is little evidence to support the view that South-South trade has become an autonomous engine of growth for developing countries. Rather, the close links between the dynamics of South-South trade, on the one hand, and trade in primary commodities and trade within international production networks whose final destination is developed-country markets, on the other, indicates that engaging in South-South trade has probably done little to reduce developing countries' vulnerability to external trade shocks.[136]

Just as during the *belle époque* European societies showed a shameful indifference to the brutal colonial practices on which their wealth was based, so today's "Information Age" is typified by narcissistic enclaves such as Silicon Valley. There, the Apple Corporation gleefully hurries forward to develop new generations of iPhones. With each new version, old models become obsolete and privileged consumers discard them. Where do these phones and other electronic gadgets end up? Much is shipped back to the periphery, to infamous e-waste dumps like Agbogbloshie in Ghana, poisoning the environment and the people, thereby completing the circuit of imperialism.[137]

THE THIRD WORLD DEBT CRISIS

So far, we have seen how U.S. politicians and corporate leaders responded to both the deteriorating value of the dollar and the decline of corporate profits in ways that contributed to the neoliberal restructuring of the global economy. Something similar happened with the Third World debt crisis, which the core countries used to impose structural adjustment measures on peripheral countries, leading to a virtual holocaust for the peoples of the Third World and a neoliberal restructuring of their economies. Any assessment of global poverty today must take these cruel measures into account, especially since the World Bank, despite its claims to the contrary, bears much responsibility for deepening global poverty through its politically motivated response to this debt crisis.

How did the current global financial architecture, in which the World Bank plays a key role, come into being? In 1944, representatives from the forty-four Allied nations met in Bretton Woods, New Hampshire, to establish the main pillars of the postwar global economy. Although delegates from the Soviet Union and some nominally independent Third World countries such as Cuba, Haiti, and Honduras were present, the U.S. government was the driving force behind the conference and its outcomes. One major agreement, discussed above, was to peg all currencies to the dollar and the dollar in turn to gold in fixed ratios. However, the Bretton Woods conference also created the International Bank for Reconstruction and Development (IRBD)—now a part of the World Bank—and the International Monetary Fund (IMF). The IRBD was designed to foster development through long-term loans to war-ravaged or impoverished countries, whereas the IMF focused on short-term loans to countries facing balance-of-payment crises. In both of these financial institutions, participating governments have decision-making power in proportion to their financial contributions. This arrangement guarantees that the U.S. government has the largest share of voting power. According to Walden Bello, "The same approach marked the establishment [in the 1950s and 1960s] of the regional banks, the African Development Bank, the Inter-American Development Bank, and Asian Development Bank—all of which guaranteed Northern hegemony by allocating influence according to the size of capital subscriptions, not membership."[138]

The core-country stranglehold on development loans did not go unchallenged. Through various initiatives, the newly independent Third World countries sought to break their control. In the late 1950s, some of these countries, together with Yugoslavia and the USSR, proposed the creation of the Special United Nations Fund for Development (SUNFED) aimed at providing a source of financing that would function as an alternative to the World Bank and corporate banks. To block this development, the World Bank created its "soft-loan" arm, the International Development Association, in 1960. Eugene Black, the U.S. banker who was president of the World Bank at the time, bluntly explained its *raison d'être*: "The International Development Association was really an idea to offset the urge for SUNFED."[139]

During this same period, the U.S. government was keenly promoting "free trade" in the world, a key milestone being the formation of the General Agreement on Tariffs and Trade (GATT) in 1947. As is the case today, the U.S. conception of free trade was limited to what serves its major corporations. When the GATT was formed, the U.S. goal was to expand its investments and secure markets for its corporations in regions previously controlled by the waning colonial powers.[140] At this time, despite U.S. efforts to extend its economic hegemony globally, China and Cuba managed to de-link from the capitalist world system, establishing more equitable trade relations with the Socialist bloc. However, most Global South countries remained trapped within the capitalist world system. Even so, many countries developed strategies of resistance. One of the most important of these strategies was "import substitution" as a development program: the idea was to build up a dependent country's productive apparatus by protecting national industries capable of supplying goods previously imported from the core countries. This strategy was widely applied across Latin America, and it led to the important, if limited industrialization of Brazil and Mexico. Another strategy was to use the state to guide and regulate economic activity, eschewing free-market doctrine in favor of a type of command capitalism. This was the strategy pursued by the Asian "newly industrialized countries" that followed Japan's lead: Hong Kong, Singapore, Taiwan, and South Korea.

The United States could tolerate some trade barriers and forms of command capitalism in the periphery. There were, however, limits to what it would accept because protectionist development strategies constrained the global expansion of its corporations and banks.[141] For this reason, the United States clashed with both Brazil and Mexico over their protectionism. Walden Bello describes how in Brazil, "where foreign-owned firms accounted for half of total manufacturing sales, the military-technocrat regime, invoking national security considerations, moved in the late 1970s to reserve the strategic information sector local industries, provoking bitter denunciation from IBM (International Business Machines) and other U.S. computer firms."[142] Likewise, U.S. pharmaceutical companies protested when the Mexican government began fostering "non-patent policies, promotion of generic medicines, local development of raw materials, price controls, discriminatory incentives for local firms and controls on foreign investment."[143] To overcome these barriers and further subordinate the peripheral countries, the U.S. government would soon leverage the Third World debt crisis of the 1980s and the East Asian financial crisis of the late 1990s into battering rams capable of demolishing most such barriers and regulations.

In this epoch, a movement in the Global South began to take shape worldwide, one that attempted to organize itself as a bloc independent of the U.S.'s imperial world system. Its emergence as an independent force was marked by a succession of conferences and summits. In 1955, government representatives from the newly independent Asian and African countries met in the Bandung Conference with a view to opposing both colonialism and neocolonialism. A year later, Gamal Abdul Nasser, Jawaharlal Nehru, and Josip Broz Tito launched the Non-Aligned Movement, which likewise pledged opposition to imperialism. This movement also made headway inside the UN. In 1964, the Group of 77 (G77) was formed at the United Nations Conference on Trade and Development, representing an alliance of peripheral governments uniting to promote their countries' collective economic interests and strengthen their voices in the United Nations. The UN General Assembly increasingly became a platform for the G77 and the Non-Aligned Movement to push for much-needed changes in the world order. A landmark achievement was the adoption of the New International Economic Order in a special session of the UN General Assembly in 1974. This proposal rejected the Bretton Woods system and called for a new global economy in which Third World governments: 1) could form trade associations along the lines of OPEC to receive higher prices for primary commodity exports; 2) regulate and even nationalize foreign corporations operating in their countries; and 3) receive genuine assistance in place of loans with strings attached. In essence, the New International Economic Order enshrined the "right of the developing countries and the peoples of territories under colonial and racial domination and foreign occupation to achieve their liberation and to regain effective control over their natural resources and economic activities."[144]

Since the United States and core-country governments controlled key institutions such as the World Bank, the G77, the OECD, and the UN Security Council (where they exercise veto power), they could contain and curtail most expressions of Global South independence. Nevertheless, Saudi Arabian complicity was important too. Walden Bello describes how the Saudi government helped sabotage OPEC's leveraging power:

> When Third World governments flocked to Paris in 1975 to confront the North at the crucial Conference on International Economic Cooperation (CIEC), many came with the expectation that the OPEC producers would stand with them to demand a comprehensive deal on a wide range of commodities. But the Saudis had been bought off: in return for allowing Saudi Arabia to purchase U.S. Treasury bills with the exact amounts kept secret, the Saudis agreed not to allow oil to be used as a weapon in the commodity conflict.[145]

Implementing the New International Economic Order would have been difficult even without Saudi betrayal. One important obstacle was the serious lack of unity among the Third World countries, many of which had become U.S. client states. Yet the Achilles' heel of the Third World movement proved to be the debt crisis that the core countries provoked and used to roll back the trade barriers developed by nationalist governments.

The roots of the Third World debt crisis go back to the unequal exchange between central and peripheral countries: low-priced primary commodities from the periphery confront the high-priced manufactures from the core countries on the international market. This unfair system and the resulting balance of payments problems drove Third World countries into the hands of Northern creditors. The situation worsened when OPEC increased the price of oil by 400 percent in the 1970s, driving up the cost of many imports for countries in the periphery. From the side of the lenders, the "special relationship" between the United States and Saudi Arabia produced a glut of dollars in the financial sector, as the Saudi monarchy and other OPEC elites began recycling their excess petrodollars not just into U.S. Treasury bonds, but also into U.S. and core country commercial banks. Since inflation and slow growth within the United States during the 1970s had made productive investment difficult, this prompted banks to loan their petrodollars to Third World governments at "teaser" interest rates. As the IMF explains on its website:

> During the 1970s, Western commercial banks had loaned billions of recycled petrodollars to the developing countries, usually at variable, or floating, interest rates. So when interest rates began to soar in 1979, the floating rates on developing countries' loans also shot up. . . . Higher interest payments are estimated to have cost the non-oil-producing developing countries at least $22 billion during 1978–81.[146]

By the early 1980s, the Third World had accrued $700 billion worth of debts to:

> American, European, and Japanese banks, which had competed intensely with one another to make loans [of petrodollars] to Southern governments in order to make profits.... Bank lending to the Third World had lost the least modicum of restraint under Citicorp chairman Walter Wriston's doctrine that, unlike individuals, "a country does not go bankrupt."[147]

Many of the countries that got caught in the debt trap were U.S. client states, with corrupt leaders who borrowed both from commercial banks and the World Bank. In fact, the World Bank's key clients in the 1970s were the biggest debtors to commercial banks.[148] Frequently, one part of the loan would find its way to private pockets, while another part would end up subsidizing the expansion of U.S. corporations.

A fraud-ridden project in Marcos's Philippines illustrates the relation between foreign loans, corruption, and imperialist influence. In 1974, General Electric applied to build a nuclear power station on the Bataan Peninsula, sixty miles from Manila. Not to be outdone by the prospect of building a nuclear reactor in an earthquake zone, Westinghouse also made a bid for the project. The Marcos dictatorship, never known for its frugality, naturally went with Westinghouse, the higher bidder. Money and permissions were easily obtained for this project. An important part of the money came from the U.S. government's Export/Import Bank, then led by William Casey (who later went on to become the director of the CIA). For its part, the U.S. State Department quickly overcame any qualms about earthquake risks and approved Westinghouse's export license. The good folks at Westinghouse responded by raising the price of the project to $2.2 billion. As one can see, money and good fortune were being shared liberally among those involved in this scheme, with the only clear losers being the Philippine people. They would someday have to pay off the huge debt, if the precariously located nuclear plant did not finish them off first.[149]

One terrible consequence of the Third World's debt bondage is that decisions made inside U.S. institutions can produce devastating crises in the periphery. That was the case with the 1981 Volcker Shock, when Federal Reserve chairman Paul Volcker decided to ramp up the federal funds rate (the interest rate at which banks that belong to the Federal Reserve system can borrow money from it) to combat rising inflation in the United States and the international depreciation of the dollar. As was intended, this move triggered a dramatic increase in overall interest rates. In fact, the Volcker Shock impacted the Third World in three ways: 1) the resulting U.S. domestic recession restricted consumer demand, drawing down the prices of Third

World exports; 2) interest rates rose on the Third World's debt, in keeping with the general increase in interest rates; and 3) most of the Third World debt was in dollars, which appreciated, making the burden on debtor countries even more crushing. Not surprisingly, the Third World debt bubble soon burst: in 1982 the Mexican government defaulted on its debt payments, and the contagion quickly spread throughout the periphery.

Since the defaults threatened U.S. banks, the Reagan administration took decisive action, using its influence in the World Bank and the IMF to guarantee huge payments and flows of wealth from the periphery to the core. During this time, a change in the World Bank's direction left Third World countries even more exposed. Robert McNamara was the World Bank president between 1968 and 1981. McNamara was no friend of humanity. Previously, as U.S. secretary of defense, he had directed the genocidal war against the Vietnamese people. Later, as the Bank's president, McNamara loaned money to corrupt regimes and facilitated the industrialization of Third World agriculture, which displaced small farmers from their land into ever-growing urban slums. However, McNamara also emphasized a soft-loan anti-poverty policy through the Bank's International Development Association. This changed in the 1980s. The new World Bank presidents, Tom Clausen and then Barber Conable, steered the Bank toward a more hard-line and disciplinary approach:

> The first salvo in this campaign [to discipline the South] was the decision to cut the U.S. promised contribution to the 1982 replenishment of the International Development Association (IDA) . . . by US$300 million. This led the other advanced countries to cut their own contributions, resulting in the soft-loan agency receiving $1 billion less than it originally expected. Since IDA loans were granted on concessional terms to the poorest countries—for example, India, other Southeast Asia countries, and African countries—the move served as a forceful signal from the Reaganites that the U.S. and its allies were "cutting off the dole." This was the first step in a process of changing the criterion

for the allocation of IDA funds from countries that needed them because they were defined as poor . . . to those that were regarded as "making the greatest efforts to restructure their economies."[150]

As part of this hard-line tendency, the World Bank and the IMF, under U.S. leadership, began imposing structural adjustment programs (SAPs) on Third World governments in return for emergency loans that allowed them to avoid default. The risks for governments that refused to implement the SAPs were extremely high; not only would they face the immediate consequences of default, but they would be isolated from other international creditors for having crossed swords with the World Bank and the IMF. Walden Bello describes the process by which structural adjustment programs became the norm during the 1980s:

> By the beginning of 1986, 12 of the 15 debtors designated by then Secretary of the Treasury James Baker as top-priority debtors— including Brazil, Mexico, Argentina, and the Philippines—had agreed to SAPs. From 3% of the total World Bank lending in 1981, structural adjustment credits rose to 19% in 1986. Five years later, the figure was 25%. By the end of 1992, about 267 SAPs had been approved. . . . Cooperation between the Bank and the Fund was brought to a higher level with the establishment in 1988 of the Structural Adjustment Facility (SAF), set up to coordinate closely the two institutions' surveillance and enforcement activities, especially in sub-Saharan Africa. Out of a total of 47 countries in that region, 36 have undergone SAPs administered by the Bank or the Fund. . . . Indeed, with over 70 Third World countries submitting to IMF and World Bank programs in the 1980s, stabilization, structural adjustment, and shock therapy managed from distant Washington became the common condition of the South in that decade.[151]

SAPs required Third World governments to 1) devalue their currencies; 2) privatize public assets; 3) remove trade and financial barriers; and 4) cut government spending on domestic programs (such as health and education) to instead service their debt obligations. It has been extensively documented how this kind of loan conditionality deepened global poverty and inequality. The number of poverty-related deaths they induced must be counted in the tens of millions.[152] Usually Third World holocausts are systematically ignored by the media. However, at the end of the1980s, as UNICEF released information about the devastating effects of cutting social spending in Asia and Africa, even the *New York Times* had to recognize the scale of the disaster:

> Half a million children died in the last 12 months because families in the developing world are sliding back into severe poverty after 40 years of progress, the United Nations Children's Fund says in its annual report.
>
> The UNICEF report, "The State of the World's Children 1989," will be released today in New Delhi.
>
> The organization found that in the last year, governments in Asia, Africa and Latin America, many falling deeper into debt, are reducing spending on services most needed by the poor. Malnutrition among children is rising in many of the countries.
>
> The report found that the world's 40 least-developed countries have cut education budgets by about 25 percent per person, and the proportion of 6- to 11-year-olds in school is falling.
>
> "The continuing economic crisis, particularly in Latin America and Africa, is really beginning to have an adverse impact on children," UNICEF's director, James P. Grant, said in an interview. "Most societies under the pressure of economic adversity have cut back disproportionately on services: health, education, social welfare programs.
>
> "More than a thousand children continue to die each day in Africa as a consequence of the economic witches' brew that flows out of low primary commodity prices, poor borrowings, high interest rates, the remaining debt crisis," said Mr. Grant, a former American aid official.[153]

Across the Third World, austerity brought hunger and disease. To take just one example, in the Philippines 44 percent of the national budget in 1992 was going toward interest payments alone on its debt, in contrast to only 3 percent on health care.[154] Similar retrenchment on health services occurred in sub-Saharan African countries, producing or at least exacerbating a rampant AIDS epidemic. How many South Africans lost their lives so that the ANC government could make payments on a debt inherited from the Apartheid period? Nor was the environment spared; Brazilian forests in the Amazon were sacrificed to pay off loans that little benefitted the Brazilian people. The voiceover in John Pilger's film *War by Other Means* graphically describes the effects of austerity policies:

> It's been described as a silent war; instead of soldiers dying, there are children dying. More than half a million in one year, according to the United Nations. That's more than twice the number of dead in the Gulf War. Instead of the bombing of bridges, there's the tearing down of forests and other natural resources, the bulldozing of farmland and the running down of schools and hospitals. In many ways it's like a colonial war. The difference these days is that people and their resources are controlled not by viceroys and their occupying armies, but by more sophisticated means of which the principal weapon is debt.[155]

Apologists of structural adjustment policies argued that, social costs notwithstanding, they made national economies more market-oriented and hence more efficient and profitable. The verdict of history, however, is otherwise. Despite the widespread application of SAPs, debt levels in the Third World kept rising in the 1980s. Kenneth Rogoff, a professor of economics at Harvard University who served on the staff of the International Monetary Fund, described the results of a decade of austerity:

> By the end of 1990 the world's poor and developing countries owed more than $1.3 trillion to industrialized countries. Among

the largest problem debtors were Brazil ($116 billion), Mexico ($97 billion), and Argentina ($61 billion). Of the total developing-country debt, roughly half is owed to private creditors, mainly commercial banks . . . The rest consists of obligations to international lending organizations such as the International Monetary Fund (IMF) and the World Bank, and to governments and government agencies—export-import banks, for example.[156]

Rogoff was writing in 1991, but the debt levels kept rising. Commercial banks were making a killing on interest payments, which quickly surpassed the principal of the loans, while Third World governments fell deeper and deeper into debt bondage. Take the case of Latin America, where interest payments siphoned off almost half of the region's GDP:

> By 1998, the total external debt in Latin America climbed to $698 billion, an increase of 64% from 1987, the peak year of the debt crisis. However, what is significant about this debt is not so much its magnitude (about 45% of regional GNP) but the sheer volume of annual interest payments made to U.S. banks, causing a huge drain of potential capital. In just one year (1995) the banks received $67.5 billion of income from this source, and over the course of the decade [1990s] well over $600 billion, a figure equivalent to around 30% of total export earnings generated over the same period, at enormous economic and social cost.[157]

As the turn of the century approached, massive protests erupted throughout the Global South demanding an end to the neocolonial world order that was now achieved through debt bondage. The protests received support from international solidarity campaigns for debt cancellation, such as Jubilee 2000. To save appearances, the World Bank and the IMF launched the Heavily Indebted Poor Countries (HIPC) Initiative in 1996 "with the aim of ensuring that no poor country faces a debt burden it cannot manage."[158] Debt relief, however, was doled out slowly and to only a few countries. Unsurprisingly, it also came with SAP-style conditions attached.

The worldwide protests continued, giving birth to what came to be called the *anti-globalization movement*. Perhaps the most emblematic protests were those that took place in Seattle in 1999, the "Battle of Seattle," but the movement soon spread to other cities. As we have seen, in 2000, the UN Millennium campaign made a call to "deal comprehensively with the debt problems of developing countries through national and international measures in order to make debt sustainable in the long term," but it refused to back full debt cancellation. Later, the G8 finance ministers launched the Multilateral Debt Relief Initiative (MDRI) in 2005. The initiative apparently allowed "for 100 percent relief on eligible debts by three multilateral institutions—the IMF, the World Bank, and the African Development Fund (AfDF)," but it required countries to complete the HIPC Initiative process.[159] An IMF document explained the conditions: "To qualify for debt relief, the IMF Executive Board also required that these countries be current on their obligations to the IMF and demonstrate satisfactory performance in macroeconomic policies, implementation of a poverty reduction strategy, and public expenditure management."[160] In essence, Third World governments would have to accept structural adjustments.

The HIPC Initiative did have some positive effects on peripheral countries. In its 2012, report *The State of Debt*, the Jubilee Debt Campaign described both the pros and cons of this kind of top-down debt relief:

> Over the last decade thirty-two countries have qualified for debt relief through HIPC. HIPC led to debt payments of many countries being reduced, from an average of 20% of government revenue in 1998 to less than 5% in 2010. Public spending on activities defined by the IMF and World Bank as reducing poverty increased, the IMF and World Bank estimate from 7% of national income in 2000 to 9% in 2009. . . . But HIPC maintained the power of creditors to tell debtors what to do. To

qualify for cancellation, countries had to implement economic conditions set by the IMF and World Bank, such as water privatization in Tanzania, or selling off grain reserves ahead of a food crisis in Malawi.[161]

The positive side of HIPC debt relief is that it allowed countries to reallocate money from debt payments to domestic services.[162] But these gains are clearly fragile, handcuffed to structural adjustment measures. What's more, many countries in the periphery never received such debt relief.

A new Third World debt crisis is on the horizon today. This time around what is driving the debt bubble is not the recycling of petrodollars, but rather the huge amounts of bailout money that commercial banks received after the 2008 financial crisis. As is well known, the U.S. government, in conjunction with other OECD governments, generously bailed out major banks and investment firms to the tune of trillions of dollars. Because credit and investment markets were weak in the core countries, the banks turned again to Third World governments, many of which needed foreign currency because of falling primary commodity prices:

> Since the start of 2014 the IMF's commodity price index has fallen by more than 40%, and the U.S. dollar has risen in value by 20%. This has caused rapidly worsening financial conditions for many countries. Using figures from the IMF and World Bank, Jubilee Debt Campaign has calculated that this has led to a group of 51 low and lower middle-income country governments being $61 billion worse off in 2016 than previously expected, due to falls in government revenue and increases in the relative size of debt payments. For comparison, this is $13 billion more than the $48 billion of aid which is claimed by the OECD to be spent in the 51 countries included in the study.[163]

Along with the commercial banks, the World Bank and IMF are once again becoming key creditors, accounting for "45% of new loans to low income countries over the last five years" (between 2007 and 2012).[164] The terms of these new loans, like previous ones, are draconian. Even at the height of the MDGs, in 2006, when the HIPC Initiative was in full swing, Third World governments were spending $25 on debt repayment for every dollar that they received in aid.[165]

Public opinion is sometimes willing to decry the world's poverty, yet it rarely dares to look for the causes. The rise of urban poverty throughout the Third World, as well as the growth of inequality between the Third and First Worlds, is no mystery. Fueling it, as we have seen above, are three major factors: the shift to an international currency regime based on floating exchange rates but with the dollar still given artificial strength; the wave of corporate outsourcing and industrial relocation from core to periphery and the formation of vast global value chains; and the Third World debt crisis, which brought with it the imposition of SAPs throughout the periphery. Taken together, these factors have profoundly shaped the world economy today. The current global order rests on huge surplus value transfers from workers in the periphery to the core countries through global value chains, repatriated profits on foreign direct investments, and debt bondage.[166]

Revolutionary leader Amilcar Cabral

4. Claim No Easy Victories, Tell No Lies

It is evident that the neoliberal growth model—upheld by the World Bank and elements of the UN establishment, the Gates and Clinton Foundations, among others—is itself a form of imperialism and is responsible for continually inflicting a "structural genocide" in the Third World while vastly deepening global inequality. Moreover, this growth model—driven as it is by the imperatives of ever-expanding capital accumulation and profit maximization—is literally destroying the ecological fabric and balance of the earth.

Recently global capitalism has been outfitted with the fig leaf of the United Nations' "Sustainable Development Goals," but the assumption that the system can be made "eco-friendly" through judicious development and applying green technologies is dangerously misleading, as many scholars, environmentalists, and scientists have demonstrated.[167] Of course, the whistleblowers have been there for a long time: indigenous leaders, activists, and social movements have all been alerting us to the dangers that come if we continue on our current course. People who are directly affected by capitalist projects, such as the Ogoni people of the Niger Delta and the Native American Peoples in Standing Rock, North Dakota, are often the first to alert us to the disastrous effects of a system driven by profit and accumulation.

What has the establishment's response been? Instead of coming to terms with these realities, neoliberal spokespeople continue to defend "trickle-down" policies that prioritize capitalist growth. They also invent narratives to lull us into complacency. Today, one of the most important of these is the story of the "miraculous" Asian economies—a "miracle" based on export-oriented growth, repression of the workforce, and integration into global value chains!—which is supposed to serve as a model for poor countries. For example, in 2016 the *Business Insider* decided to lecture Africans, as Bill Gates had done previously,[168] to follow the Asian example:

> The point is that a colonial past is no excuse for Africa's failure so far to catch up, emulate and leapfrog. . . . Very few nations prosper without well-organized and strategically focused hard work and sacrifice. Africans need to learn to direct effort and resources with a long-term goal. Leadership is key.[169]

The Asian success narrative is like the old Horatio Alger rags-to-riches stories, now updated to be about nations rather than individuals. Today this fairy-tale perspective has also entered the academic world. For example, Steven Radelet at Georgetown University has joined the chorus of those lecturing Third World governments on the market-friendly policies and "good governance" that is required for success. Radelet's comments are egregious for their superficiality and especially for overlooking the role of U.S. imperialism. Haiti, he says, "has moved forward since the repressive days of the Duvaliers but continues to suffer from massive governance failures."[170] This statement is truly extraordinary. One wonders whether the 2004 U.S.-orchestrated coup against Jean-Bertrand Aristide qualifies as one of the "governance failures."

The "Asian miracle" narrative also has an unfortunate similarity to the "model minority" stereotype that the United States establishment promoted in the 1960s and 1970s to lecture non-Asian minorities on how to be successful and realize the American dream. Both narratives aim to short-circuit questioning of unjust power structures and block substantial systemic change. It may be politically convenient to lecture Third World countries about the need to climb the global ladder and emulate the Asian "miracle" economies—combining the right mix of state intervention and free market policies—but these prescriptions ignore the real basis of such economic "miracles." Not only do they depend on intense labor exploitation and repression (particularly of women). They also hinge on the dispossession of indigenous peoples and wanton environmental destruction.[171]

The Shanghai and Chongqing skylines are perhaps the most widely disseminated images of the new China. Yet behind these shining boom cities is a huge environmental catastrophe. As Hart-Landsberg explains:

> The country's industrialization has had devastating environmental consequences. For example, the World Health Organization (WHO)–supported study "found outdoor air pollution contributed to 1.2 million premature deaths in China, accounting for 40% of the global total." More than 70% of China's lakes and rivers are polluted, with almost 40% of those considered seriously polluted. The WHO estimates that some 100,000 people die each year from water pollution-related illnesses. At least a hundred million people a year are sickened from bacterial foodborne diseases caused by a lack of regulation and contaminated agricultural land; Chinese researchers believe that close to 70% of China's farmland is contaminated with toxic chemicals.[172]

The water in China's rivers and lakes is now largely undrinkable, and environmental illnesses cause up to 300,000 deaths annually. Although it may be problematic to assign a monetary value to such damage, the vice-minister of China's State Environmental Protection Administration estimates the annual environmental damage to be in the range of 8 to 13 percent of China's GDP, which offsets all of China's growth since the 1970s.[173] Much of the pollution comes from factories where super-exploited workers produce electronic devices, such as iPhones, destined for U.S. markets. This, then, is the wonderful example that neoliberal enthusiasts advocate for developing countries.

If the Asian Miracle path is a chimera, what options remain for Third World countries? The truth is that mere policy fixes cannot resolve the humanitarian and environmental crisis that the world faces today, produced by the contradictions of capitalism in both the periphery and core. Capitalism cannot be tamed to make it either sustainable or humanly acceptable. Perhaps the capitalist system can be extended further into the periphery and new "miracle" economies could arise and multiply, as Radelet and the World Bank envision. But capitalism's inexorable polarizing tendency would persist, producing more poor people and underdeveloped countries than rich ones.

The damage that the capitalist world system does to people's material well-being is only part of the picture. Capitalism also severely truncates human freedom and personal development. The dominant capitalist culture equates freedom with being "free" to compete, to amass property and wealth with no limits. But freedom can better be envisioned and experienced as a process of embracing and being embraced by others as true equals, of consciously working together to create conditions in which all people have the ability to develop their potential and interests, all the while respecting nature. Che Guevara's internationalism and Paulo Freire's popular pedagogy would be stellar examples of this kind of freedom. It can be thought of as both an *end* and a *means:* the practice of building solidarity near and far in the struggle to replace capitalism with a cooperative, ecological way of living.

Now is the time to fortify revolutionary movements and grassroots organizations across the world. These movements address varied aspects of the capitalist crisis and can take quite different forms. Fanmi Lavalas in Haiti is a political party, whereas the Landless Workers Movement in Brazil (MST) is a huge social movement. Despite claims that the proletariat has disappeared, workers' struggles are still quite alive. Not surprisingly, they are powerful in China's highly industrialized economy, involving both unionized and non-unionized workers. In India, armed community resistance to hydroelectric and mining projects takes place throughout the huge regions under Maoist influence. In the United States, promising struggles have emerged in the Black Lives Matter movement and the Standing Rock Sioux resistance to the building of a gas pipeline. We should always keep in mind that a great many struggles by workers, peasants, and impoverished people never make it into mass media headlines.

Given the gravity of the crisis, it is necessary to move from a defensive to an offensive posture, forging regional, national, and international platforms linking these struggles. The goal should be to accumulate force and share conceptions of sustainable postcapitalist scenarios. While some may label this perspective "ultra-left" or "utopian," it is far more realistic than attempting to make capitalism into a system compatible with human liberation and meaningful democracy. There is no need to underestimate the challenges. Amilcar Cabral, the revolutionary leader from Guinea-Bissau, once advised that we should "claim no easy victories, tell no lies," all the while struggling relentlessly to build a new society based upon true power by, of, and for the people. Unflinching honesty and commitment of the kind that Cabral showed are more than ever needed in the world today.

Notes

1. The U.S. role is well documented. For example, see Paul Farmer, *The Uses of Haiti* (Monroe, ME: Common Courage Press, 2006); and Randall Robinson, *An Unbroken Agony: Haiti, from Revolution to the Kidnapping of a President* (New York: Basic Civitas Books, 2008).

2. For thorough, unrelenting documentation of the UN role in this brutal repression, see the documentary film *Haiti: We Must Kill the Bandits,* Haiti Information Project, 2009.

3. To gain a sense of the scale of the violence, see the excellent reports *Hidden from the Headlines: The U.S. War Against Haiti* (Berkeley: Haiti Action Committee, 2004); and Thomas Griffin, *Haiti Human Rights Investigation: November 11–21* (Miami, FL: Center for the Study of Human Rights, University of Miami School of Law, 2004).

4. See our report *Growing Evidence of a Massacre by UN Occupation Forces in Port-au-Prince Neighborhood of Cité Soleil: A Summary of Findings of the U.S. Labor and Human Rights Delegation to Haiti* (July 12, 2005).

5. For a full list of targets and indicators, see UNICEF, *Millennium Development Goals* (MDG) *Monitoring* https://www.unicef.org/statistics/index_24304.html.

6. OECD, *The OECD and the Millennium Development Goals,* http://www.oecd.org/dev/The%20OECD%20and%20the%20Millennium%20Development%20Goals.pdf.

7. Samir Amin, "The Millennial Goals:: A Critique from the South," *Monthly Review* 57/10 (March 2006). Similar concerns are raised by Antonio Tujan, chairperson of the International Management Committee of the Reality of Aid Network, in a 2004 presentation titled *The Millennium Development Goals: Reducing Poverty or Deodorizing Neoliberal Globalization?*, http://www.rorg.no/Artikler/717.html.

8. In its 2016 *State of the World's Children* report, UNICEF estimates that 5 million children below five are dying each year due to "inequity." An estimate by Dr. Gideon Polya places the total number of preventable deaths due to poverty-related conditions each year at 17 million. See Share the World's Resources, "Beyond the Sustainable Development Goals: Uncovering the Truth about Global Poverty and Demanding the Universal Realisation of Article 25," https://www.sharing.org/information-centre/reports/beyond-sustainable-development-goals-uncovering-truth-about-global#The%20 hidden%20emergency%20of%20preventable%20deaths._ Also see Gary Leech, *Capitalism: A Structural Genocide* (London: Zed Press, 2012).

9. Global Issues, "Poverty Facts and Stats," http://www.globalissues.org/article/26/poverty-facts-and-stats.

10. That percentage is said to be 12.9 percent, but it contradicts the World Food Programme's estimate that approximately 33 percent of the world is suffering today from some form of malnutrition. United Nations, *The Millennium Development Goals Report 2015* (New York: United Nations, 2015), 4.

11. World Bank, "World Bank Forecasts Global Poverty to Fall Below 10% for First Time; Major Hurdles Remain in Goal to End Poverty by 2030," October 4, 2015, 7.

12. World Bank, "Understanding Poverty," http://www.worldbank.org/en/understanding-poverty.

13. World Bank, "The World by Income, FY2017," http://datatopics.worldbank.org/sdgatlas/archive/2017/the-world-by-income.html.

14. "Not Always with Us," *The Economist,* June 1, 2013.

15. World Bank, "FAQs: Global Poverty Line Update," http://www.worldbank.org/en/topic/poverty/brief/global-poverty-line-faq. Emphasis mine.

16. UNCTAD, *Growth and Poverty Eradication: Why Addressing Inequality Matters*, November 2013, http://unctad.org/en/PublicationsLibrary/press-pb2013d4_en.pdf. Emphasis mine.

17. Jason Hickel, "Could You Live on $1.90 a Day? That's the International Poverty Line." *The Guardian,* November 1, 2015.

18. Ibid.

19. Rakesh Kochhar, "A Global Middle Class Is More Promise than Reality." *Pew Research Center's Global Attitudes Project,* June 14, 2018.

20. See http://iresearch.worldbank.org/PovcalNet/methodology.aspx.

21. John Smith, *Imperialism in the Twenty-First Century* (New York: Monthly Review Press, 2016), 340.

22. For solid information on realities of economic insecurity and exploitation in post-Mao China, see Mobo Gao, *The Battle for China's Past: Mao and the Cultural Revolution* (London: Pluto Press, 2008); Martin Hart-Landsberg, "The Chinese Reform Experience: A Critical Assessment," *Review of Radical Political Economics* 43/1(Winter 2011); Martin Hart-Landsberg, "The Realities of China Today." *Against the Current* 137 (November–December 2008); Paul Burkett and Martin Hart-Landsberg, "China and Socialism,

Market Reforms and Class Struggle," *Monthly Review* 56/3 (July–August 2004). Also see http://chinalaborwatch.org/home.aspx.

23. Also, see Michael D. Yates, "Measuring Global Inequality," *Monthly Review* 68/6 (November 2016). Here Yates states that "while money incomes are higher for peasants in China than they were before its leaders pushed it sharply toward capitalism, more than 600 million rural residents have lost their communal lands and their collectively provided food rations and medical care, none of which is subtracted from their current money incomes." Also, see Zhun Xu, *From Commune to Capitalism: How China's Peasants Lost Collective Farming and Gained Urban Poverty* (New York: Monthly Review Press, 2018).

24. World Bank, "The International Poverty Line Has Just Been Raised to $1.90 a Day, but Global Poverty Is Basically Unchanged. How Is That Even Possible?," http://blogs.worldbank.org/developmenttalk/international-poverty-line-has-just-been-raised-190-day-global-poverty-basically-unchanged-how-even.

25. Jason Hickel argues that $1.92 a day would have preserved the original value of the existing poverty line. Yet this would have shown an increase in world poverty. So it was revised downward by two cents. Jason Hickel, "Could You Live on $1.90 a Day? That's the International Poverty Line," *The Guardian*. November 1, 2015, https://www.theguardian.com/global-development-professionals-network/2015/nov/01/global-poverty-is-worse-than-you-think-could-you-live-on-190-a-day.

26. World Bank, "International Comparison Program (ICP)," http://www.worldbank.org/en/programs/icp#6.

27. For a clear explanation of this process, see Gernot Kohler and Arno Tausch, *Global Keynesianism and Unequal Exchange* (New York: Nova Science Publishers, 2002), 46–49.

28. World Bank Group, *Purchasing Power Parities and the Real Size of World Economies: A Comprehensive Report of the 2011 International Comparison Program*, http://pubdocs.worldbank.org/en/142181487105157824/ICP-2011-report.pdf, 33.

29. For a thorough examination of this discrepancy between PPP and market exchange rates, see Gernot Kohler and Arno Tausch, *Global Keynesianism: Unequal Exchange and Global Exploitation*, 43–59.

30. Ibid., 49.

31. World Bank, "PPP Conversion Factor, Private Consumption (LCU per International $)," https://data.worldbank.org/indicator/PA.NUS.PRVT.PP?locations=HT.

32. Aseem Shrivastava, "India on 20 Cents a Day," *CounterPunch*, January 28, 2016, https://www.counterpunch.org/2006/11/25/india-on-20-cents-a-day/.

33. Angus Deaton and Bettina Aten, "Trying to Understand the PPPs in ICP 2011: Why Are the Results So Different?," *National Bureau of Economic Research* (issued in June 2014 and updated in April 2015), 2.

34. Karen Deep Singh, "India's Growth Is Helping Reduce the Number of Poor in South Asia, World Bank Says," *Wall Street Journal,* October 4, 2016. https://blogs.wsj.com/indiarealtime/2016/10/04/indias-growth-is-helping-reduce-the-number-of-poor-in-south-asia-world-bank-says/.

35. Reuters, "Nearly 80 Pct of India Lives on Half Dollar a Day," August 10, 2007, http://www.reuters.com/article/idUSDEL218894.

36. Ibid.

37. National Commission of Enterprises in the Organized Sector, *Report on Conditions of Work and Promotion of Livelihoods in the Unorganised Sector,* September 2007.

38. See for example, C. P. Chandrasekhar, "Chronic Famishment," *MacroScan,* February 21, 2012, www.macroscan.org/cur/feb12/cur210212Chronic_Famishment.htm; Jayati Ghosh, "Once More without Feeling: The Government of India's Latest Poverty Estimates," *MacroScan,* August, 2013, http://www.macroscan.org/cur/aug13/pdf/Poverty_Estimates.pdf; and Rahul Goswami, "The India Behind the New Poverty Ratio," *MacroScan,* July 2013, http://www.macroscan.org/cur/jul13/pdf/Poverty_Ratio.pdf.

39. Orlan Ryan and agencies, "Food Riots Grip Haiti," *The Guardian,* April 9, 2008.

40. NBC Universal News Group, "Haiti's Poor Resort to Eating Mud as Prices Rise," January 29, 2008, www.nbcnews.com/id/22902512/ns/world_news-americas/t/haitis-poor-resort-eating-mud-prices-rise/#.WXEKXRXysdU.

41. Smith, *Imperialism in the Twenty-First Century,* 140.

42. Sanjay Reddy and Thomas Pogge, "How Not to Count the Poor," *Initiative for Policy Dialogue Working Papers Series,* May 2009, 26.

43. Sanjay Reddy and Rahul Lahoti, "$1.90 a Day: What Does It Say?" (October 6, 2015, version), 11, https://www.ineteconomics.org/uploads/general/WBPovBlogOct6PostinFinal.pdf.

44. Sanjay Reddy and Thomas Pogge, "How Not to Count the Poor," 21.

45. Quoted in Smith, *Imperialism in the Twenty-First Century,* 139.

46. Sanjay Reddy and Rahul Lahot, "$1.90 a Day: What Does It Say?," *New Left Review* (January–February, 2016): 5.

47. Ibid., 5.

48. Ibid., 6.

49. Alan Freeman, "The Poverty of Statistics," *Munich Personal RePEc Archive* (December 1, 2008): 4.

50. Ibid, 8.

51. Sanjay Reddy and Rahul Lahot, "$1.90 a Day: What Does It Say?" *New Left Review* (January–February, 2016), 2.

52. Sanjay Reddy and Thomas Pogge, "How Not to Count the Poor," 26.

53. See Robert Ackland, Steve Dowrick, and Benoit Freyens, "Measuring Global Poverty: Why PPP Methods Matter," *Review of Economics and Statistics* 95/3 (July 2013): 813–24.

54. Ibid.

55. Tami Luhby, "71% Of the World's Population Lives on Less than $10 a Day," *CNNMoney,* July 8, 2015, https://money.cnn.com/2015/07/08/news/economy/global-low-income/index.html.

56. Jason Hickel et al., "3 Ways Humans Create Poverty," *Fast Company,* March 13, 2015, www.fastcompany.com/3043284/3-ways-humans-create-poverty.

57. Rakesh Kochhar, "A Global Middle Class Is More Promise than Reality," *Pew Research Center's Global Attitudes Project,* June 14, 2018.

58. Michael Forsythe, "China's Billionaire People's Congress Makes Capitol Hill Look Like Pauper," Bloomberg News, February 27, 2012, quoted in Martin Hart-Landsberg, "From the Claw to the Lion: A Critical Look at Capitalist Globalization," *Critical Asian Studies* 47/1 (March 2015): 14.

59. Rakesh Kochhar, "A Global Middle Class Is More Promise than Reality."

60. Martin Hart-Landsberg, "From the Claw to the Lion," 15.

61. Steven C. Radelet, *The Great Surge: The Ascent of the Developing World* (New York: Simon & Schuster, 2016), 41.

62. Sabina Alkire and Gisela Robles, *Global Multidimensional Poverty Index 2017* (Oxford: Oxford Poverty and Human Development Initiative, 2017); see p. 3 for the list of categories and indicators. Like the World Bank's international poverty line, the MPI Initiative provides poverty headcounts. But it also considers the intensity of poverty in each country (the average percentage of deprivation in each of the three categories of health, education, and living standard of those poor people). The MPI per se for a country is the percentage of poor people multiplied by the intensity of their deprivation.

63. Ibid., 1.

64. Ibid., 6.

65. Ibid., 4.

66. Jason Hickel, "The True Extent of Global Poverty and Hunger: Questioning the Good News Narrative of the Millennium Development Goals," *Third World Quarterly* 37/5 (2016): 749–67.

67. Ibid.

68. Ibid.

69. Ibid.

70. Ibid.

71. Steven Radelet, *The Great Surge: The Ascent of the Developing World*, p. 73.

72. Ibid., 161.

73. Ibid., 173.

74. United Nations, The *Millennium Development Goals Report 2015* (New York: United Nations, July 2015), 6.

75. To give a sense of scale of the Gates Foundation's aid: "In total it has disbursed over $26 billion, most of it to global health. To put these figures into perspective: since 1914 the Rockefeller Foundation has given $14 billion (adjusted to today's values). Only the U.S. and British governments give more to global health today. The World Health Organization (WHO), meanwhile, operates on less than $2 billion a year." See https://newint.org/features/2012/04/01/bill-gates-charitable-giving-ethics.

76. "Microsoft lobbied vociferously for the World Trade Organization's TRIPS agreement (the agreement on trade-related aspects of intellectual property), which obliges member countries to defend patents for a minimum of 20 years after the filing date. As recently as 2007, Microsoft was lobbying the G8 to tighten global intellectual property (IP) protection, a move that would, Oxfam said, 'worsen the health crisis in developing countries.'" See https://newint.org/features/2012/04/01/bill-gates-charitable-giving-ethics.

77. Greg Palast, "Killing Africans for Profit and PR. Mr. Bush's Bogus AIDS Offer," *Bigeye.com,* July 14 ,2003, https://www.bigeye.com/billgates.htm.

78. UNICEF, *The State of the World's Children 2016* (New York: UNICEF, June 2016), https://www.unicef.org/publications/files/UNICEF_SOWC_2016.pdf, 3.

79. Share the World's Resources, "Beyond the Sustainable Development Goals: Uncovering the Truth about Global Poverty and Demanding the Universal Realisation of Article 25," https://www.sharing.org/information-centre/reports/beyond-sustainable-development-goals-uncovering-truth-about-global#The%20hidden%20emergency%20of%20preventable%20death.

80. Radelet, *The Great Surge: the Ascent of the Developing World*, 74.

81. Simon Rogers, "Maternal Mortality: How Many Women Die in Childbirth in Your Country?" *The Guardian,* April 13, 2010, https://www.theguardian.com/news/datablog/2010/apr/12/maternal-mortality-rates-millennium-development-goals.

82. World Bank, *Haiti Improves Access to Education with a Targeted Government Strategy,* November 21, 2012, http://www.worldbank.org/en/news/feature/2012/11/21/haiti-education-strategy.

83. My own interviews in Port-au-Prince with Haitian educators and activists—who will remain anonymous here for safety purposes—portrayed quite a different reality than that alleged by the Martelly regime.

84. UNICEF, *State of the World's Children 2016*, 42.

85. United Nations Human Settlements Programme (UN-Habitat), *World Cities Report 2016—Urbanization and Development: Emerging Futures* (Nairobi: UN-Habitat, 2016), 3. Emphasis mine.

86. For documentation of this displacement, see Robert Richter, *Hungry for Profit* (PBS 1985); Frederick H. Buttel, Fred Magdoff, and John Bellamy Foster, eds., *Hungry for Profit: The Agribusiness Threat to Farmers, Food, and the Environment* (New York: Monthly Review Press, 2000); Roger Burback and Patricia Flynn, *Agribusiness in the Americas* (New York: Monthly Review Press, 1980); Alexander Reid Ross, ed., *Grabbing Back: Essays Against the Global Land Grab* (Oakland, CA: AK Press, 2014); Mike Davis, *Planet of Slums* (London: Verso, 2017); and the many books by Vandana Shiva on the subject.

87. Philip McMichael, "The World Food Crisis in Historical Perspective," *Monthly Review* 61/3 (July–August 2009).

88. Davis, *Planet of Slums, 23.*

89. Ibid.

90. As quoted by Immanuel Ness, *Southern Insurgency: The Coming of the Global Working Class* (London: Pluto Press, 2016), 15.

91. Garry Leech, "Distorting Poverty to Promote Capitalism," *CounterPunch,* October 30, 2014, https://www.counterpunch.org/2014/01/29/distorting-poverty-to -promote-capitalism/.

92. Ben Selwyn gives a good example of this sugarcoating when he quotes Jeffrey Sachs, UN Millennium Project director, saying that "sweatshops are the first rung on the ladder out of extreme poverty." Ben Selwyn,"Development by the Elites, For the Elites," *CounterPunch,* November 10, 2014, https://www.counterpunch.org/2014/03/07/development-by-the-elites-for-the-elites/.

93. Michael Yates, "Measuring Global Inequality," *Monthly Review* 68/6 (November 2016).

94. BBC News, "China Tops U.S. in Numbers of Billionaires," October 13, 2016, http://www.bbc.com/news/business-37640156.

95. "India's 100 Richest People," *Forbes, 2018 Ranking,* https://www.forbes.com/india-billionaires/list/#tab:overall.

96. Jason Hickel, *The Divide: A Brief Guide to Global Inequality and Its Solutions* (London: Penguin Random House, 2017), 53–54.

97. Jason Hickel, "Global Inequality May Be Much Worse than We Think," *The Guardian,* April 8, 2016, https://www.theguardian.com/global-development-professionals-network/2016/apr/08/global-inequality-may-be-much-worse-than-we-think. For a more in-depth analysis of global inequality, see Hickel's *The Great Divide: A Brief Guide to Global Inequality and Its Solutions.*

98. Oxfam Briefing Paper, *An Economy for the 1%: How Privilege and Power Drive Extreme Inequality and How This Can Be Stopped* (Oxford: Oxfam GB, January 18, 2016), 2.

99. For example, see David Harvey, *Brief History of Neoliberalism* (Oxford: Oxford University Press, 2007); Atilio Boron, *State, Capitalism and Democracy in Latin America* (Boulder, CO: Lynne Rienner, 1995).

100. For thorough information on this history and these relationships, see Harry Magdoff, *The Age of Imperialism: The Economics of U.S. Foreign Policy* (New York: Monthly Review Press, 1969); Eduardo Galeano, *The Open Veins of Latin America: Five Centuries of the Pillage of a Continent* (New York: Monthly Review Press, 1971); Walter Rodney, *How Europe Underdeveloped Africa* (London: Bogle-L'Ouverture Publications, 1972); Eric Williams, *Capitalism and Slavery* (Chapel Hill: University of North Carolina Press, 1944); Edward E. Baptist, *The Half Has Never Been Told: Slavery and the Making of American Capitalism* (New York: Basic Books, 2014); Maria Mies, *Patriarchy and Accumulation on a World Scale* (London: Zed Press, 1986); Paul A. Baran, *The Political Economy of Growth* (New York: Monthly Review Press, 1957); Andre Gunder Frank, *The Development of Underdevelopment* (New York: Monthly Review Press, 1966); Samir Amin, *Unequal Development: An Essay on the Social*

Formations of Peripheral Capitalism (New York: Monthly Review Press, 1977); Arghiri Emmanuel, *Unequal Exchange: A Study of the Imperialism of Trade* (New York: Monthly Review Press, 1972); Immanuel Wallerstein, *The Capitalist World-Economy* (Cambridge: Cambridge University Press, 1979); Ernest Mandel, *An Introduction to Marxist Economic Theory,* vol. 1 (New York: Monthly Review Press, 1962); Zak Cope, *Divided World, Divided Class: Global Political Economy and the Stratification of Labor under Capitalism* (Oakland, CA: AK Press, 2012); Zak Cope, *The Wealth of (Some) Nations: Imperialism and the Mechanics of Value Transfer* (London: Pluto Press, 2019); Butch Lee and Red Rover, *Night Vision: Illuminating War and Class on the Neo-Colonial Terrain* (New York: Vagabond Press, 1993); Vijay Prashad, *The Poorer Nations: A Possible History of the Global South* (London: Verso, 2014); Jason Hickel, *The Divide: A Brief Guide to Global Inequality and Its Solutions* (London: Penguin Random House UK, 2017); and Benjamin Selwyn, *The Struggle for Development* (Malden, MA: Polity Press, 2017).

101. Noam Chomsky has reviewed these documents, such as George Kennan's State Department memo PPS23, and discusses them extensively in his many books. Also, see Laurence Shoup, *Imperial Brain Trust: The Council on Foreign Relations and U.S. Foreign Policy* (New York: Monthly Review Press, 1977). For an in-depth overview and analysis of U.S. imperialism during this phase and beyond, see Harry Magdoff, *The Age of Imperialism: The Economics of US Foreign Policy* (New York: Monthly Review Press, 1969).

102. See William Blum, *Killing Hope: U.S. Military and CIA interventions Since WWII* (Monroe, ME: Common Courage Press, 2004).

103. For perhaps the best overview of this network of client regimes and analysis of their function, see Noam Chomsky and Edward Herman, *The Washington Connection to Third World Fascism* (Boston: South End Press, 1979); also Edward Herman, *The Real Terror Network* (Boston: South End Press, 1982).

104. Richard Nixon, "Address to the Nation Outlining a New Economic Policy: 'The Challenge of Peace,'" American Presidency Project, August 15, 1971, https://www.presidency.ucsb.edu/documents/address-the-nation-outlin-ing-new-economic-policy-the-challenge-peace#axzz1UZnES7PMon.

105. Comptroller General of the United States, *The US-Saudi Arabian Joint Commission on Economic Cooperation* (Washington, D.C.: Comptroller General of the United States, March 22, 1979), https://www.gao.gov/assets/130/126054.pdf.

106. Greg Grandin, "Kissinger Poisoned the Middle East: America Is Living in the Quagmire of His Making," *Salon,* September 30, 2015, http://www.salon.com/2015/09/30/kissinger_poisoned_the_middle_east_america_is_living_in_a_quagmire_of_his_making_partner/.

107. See this insightful interview with Chomsky for more info on the embargo and U.S. imperialism: https://chomsky.info/197703/.

108. Martin Hart-Landsberg, *Capitalist Globalization: Consequences, Resistance, and Alternatives* (New York: Monthly Review Press, 2013), 15.

109. Ibid., 16.

110. Martin Hart-Landsberg, *Capitalist Globalization: Consequences, Resistance, and Alternatives* (New York: Monthly Review Press, 2013), 15.

111. John Bellamy Foster, "Intro: the New Imperialism of Globalized Monopoly Finance Capital," *Monthly Review*, 67/3 (July–August, 2015).

112. John Smith, *Imperialism in the Twenty-First Century*, 55.

113. Ibid., 49.

114. "The current centrality of the Third World to transnational production is highlighted by the fact that in 2010, for the first time ever, more than half of all FDI went to Third World and transition economies." Martin Hart-Landsberg, *Capitalist Globalization*, 18–19.

115. Smith, *Imperialism in the Twenty-First Century*, 73.

116. UNCTAD, *World Investment Report 2013* (Geneva: United Nations Publications, 2013), x.

117. Ibid., 122.

118. Ibid., 136.

119. As quoted in Hart-Landsberg, "From the Claw to the Lion," 5.

120. Ibid, 5.

121. Steve Schaefer, "The World's Largest Companies 2016," *Forbes*, May 25, 2016, https://www.forbes.com/sites/steveschaefer/2016/05/25/the-worlds-largest-companies-2016/#3e1aa3c645a6.

122. Hart-Landsberg, "From the Claw to the Lion," 6–7.

123. N. B. Turner, *Is China an Imperialist Country? Considerations and Evidence* (Montreal: Kersplebedeb Publishing, 2015), 101.

124. Patrick Bond and Ana Garcia, eds., *Brazil, Russia, India, South Africa: An Anti-Capitalist Critique* (London: Pluto Press, 2015), 1.

125. Ibid., 2.

126. "China Establishes Rival to World Bank," *The Telegraph*, December 25, 2015, http://www.telegraph.co.uk/finance/newsbysector/banksandfinance/12069026/China-establishes-rival-to-World-Bank.html.

127. Ibid., 1.

128. For a strong survey of the impact of this "extractive" imperialism in Latin America, see Henry Veltmeyer and James Petras, eds., *The New Extractivism: A Post-Neoliberal Development Model or Imperialism of the Twenty-First Century?* (London: Zed Books, 2014).

129. UNCTAD, *Trade and Development Report, 2013* (New York and Geneva: United Nations Publications, 2013), 60. http://unctad.org/en/PublicationsLibrary/tdr2013_en.pdf.

130. Yanis Varoufakis, *The Global Minotaur: America, Europe and the Future of the Global Economy*, 2nd ed. (London: Zed Books, 2015).

131. UNCTAD, *Trade and Development Report, 2010*, quoted in Hart-Landsberg, "From the Claw to the Lion," 11.

132. Remy Herrera, "Dollar Imperialism, 2015 Edition," *CounterPunch*, March

10, 2015, https://www.counterpunch.org/2015/03/06/dollar-imperialism -2015-edition/.

133. Quoted in Smith, *Imperialism in the Twenty First-Century*, 45.

134. Hart-Landsberg, "From the Claw to the Lion," 7.

135. For an excellent summation of the intersections between neoliberalism and neocolonialism, see Butch Lee and Red Rover, *Night Vision: Illuminating War and Class on the Neo-Colonial Terrain* (New York: Vagabond Press, 1993).

136. UNCTAD, *Trade and Development Report, 2013*, 29.

137. John Vidal, "Toxic 'e-Waste' Dumped in Poor Nations, Says United Nations," *The Guardian*, December 14, 2013, https://www.theguardian. com/global-development/2013/dec/14/toxic-ewaste-illegal-dumping -developing-countries.

138. Walden Bello, *Dark Victory: The United States, Structural Adjustment, and Global Poverty* (Oakland, CA: Institute for Food and Development Policy, 1994), 11.

139. Ibid., 11.

140. For a thorough analysis of this post–Second World War phase of U.S. impe- rialism, see Harry Magdoff, *The Age of Imperialism*.

141. The reasons for the "exception" of East Asia are discussed extensively by Walden Bello in his book *Dragons in Distress: Asia's Miracle Economies in Crisis* (Oakland, CA: Institute for Food and Development, 1990). Also see Martin Hart-Landsberg and Paul Burkett, "East Asia and the Crisis of Development Theory," *Journal of Contemporary Asia* 28/4 (1998).

142. Bello, *Dark Victory*, 15–16.

143. Ibid.

144. United Nations General Assembly, *Declaration on the Establishment of a New International Economic Order*, May 1, 1974, http://www.un-docu- ments.net/s6r3201.htm.

145. Bello, *Dark Victory*, 24.

146. International Monetary Fund, "Debt and Transition (1981–1989)," https:// www.imf.org/external/np/exr/center/mm/eng/mm_dt_01.htm.

147. Bello, *Dark Victory*, 25.

148. Ibid., 15.

149. Investigative journalist and filmmaker John Pilger depicts this scam in his powerful 1992 film *War by Other Means*, which deals with the World Bank and the IMF. John Perkins's book *Confessions of an Economic Hit Man* (Oakland, CA: Berrett-Koehler Publishers, 2004) provides many other similar examples.

150. Bello, *Dark Victory*, 26.

151. Ibid., 30–31.

152. The literature on the genocidal impact of the Washington Consensus is extensive. In addition to *Dark Victory* by Walden Bello, see, for example, Asad Ismi, *Impoverishing a Continent: The World Bank and the IMF in Africa* (Canada: Halifax Initiative, 2004); Gloria T. Emeagwali, ed., *Women*

Pay the Price: Structural Adjustment in Africa and the Caribbean (Trenton, NJ: Africa World Press, 1995); reports by Food First: Institute for Food and Development and Oxfam International; and UNICEF's *State of the World's Children* reports from the 1980s.

153. Barbara Crossette, "Unicef Says Third World Children Are Dying as Development Falters," *New York Times,* December 20, 1988, https://www.nytimes.com/1988/12/20/world/unicef-says-third-world-children-are-dying-as-development-falters.html.

154. Pilger, *War by Other Means.*

155. Ibid.

156. Kenneth Rogoff, "Third World Debt," *Concise Encyclopedia of Economics, Library of Economics and Liberty* (1991), http://www.econlib.org/library/Enc1/ThirdWorldDebt.html.

157. Data is from World Bank. James Petras and Henry Veltmeyer, *Globalization Unmasked: Imperialism in the 21st Century* (London: Zed Books, 2001), 78–79.

158. International Monetary Fund, *Fact Sheet: Debt Relief Under the Heavily Indebted Poor Countries Initiative,* March 19, 2019, http://www.imf.org/en/About/Factsheets/Sheets/2016/08/01/16/11/Debt-Relief-Under-the-Heavily -Indebted-Poor-Countries-Initiative.

159. Ibid.

160. International Monetary Fund, *Fact Sheet: The Multilateral Debt Relief Initiative,* https://www.imf.org/external/np/exr/facts/mdri.htm.

161. Jubilee Debt Campaign, *The State of Debt* (London: Jubilee Debt Campaign, 2012), 6.

162. Ibid., "Key Facts" section.

163. Jubilee Debt Campaign, *The New Developing World Debt Crisis* (November, 2016), 2.

164. Jubilee Debt Campaign, *The State of Debt,* 6.

165. Anup Shah, "Poverty Facts and Stats," *Global Issues: Social, Political, Economic, and Environmental Issues That Affect Us All,* http://www.global-issues.org/article/26/poverty-facts-and-stats#src22.

166. For detailed analysis and estimates on this drain of wealth from the periphery to the core, see John Smith, *Imperialism in the 21st Century*; Jason Hickel, "The True Extent of Global Poverty and Hunger: Questioning the Good News Narrative of the Millennium Development Goals"; and Zak Cope, *Divided World, Divided Class* and *The Wealth of (Some) Nations*; and the recent report by Jubilee Debt Campaign, *Honest Accounts 2017: How the World Profits from Africa's Wealth.*

167. For example, see Fred Magdoff and John Bellamy Foster, *What Every Environmentalist Needs to Know About Capitalism* (New York: Monthly Review Press, 2011); Richard Smith, *Green Capitalism: The God that Failed* (London: College Publications, 2016); Naomi Klein, *This Changes Everything: Capitalism vs. the Climate* (New York: Simon & Schuster, 2014); Paul Burkett, "An Eco-Revolutionary Tipping Point?," *Monthly Review* 69/1 (May 2017).

168. Bill Gates, "Can the Asian Miracle Happen in Africa?," *Gatesnotes.com,* December 8, 2014, https://www.gatesnotes.com/Books/How-Asia-Works.

169. Sandile Swana and Lumkile Mondi, "Here's What It Will Take for African Countries to Emulate the 'Asian Miracle,'" *Business Insider,* July 12, 2016, http://www.businessinsider.com/heres-what-it-will-take-for-african-countries-to-emulate-the-asian-miracle-2016-7?pundits_only=0&get_all_comments=1&no_reply_filter=1.

170. Radelet, *The Great Surge: The Ascent of the Developing World,* 114.

171. For more information on these dynamics, see Walden Bello and Stephanie Rosenfeld, *Dragons in Distress: Asia's Miracle Economies in Crisis*; Martin-Hart Landsberg and Paul Burkett, "Contradictions of Capitalist Industrialization in East Asia: A Critique of 'Flying Geese' Theories of Development," *Economic Geography* 74/2 (April 1998); and David McNally, "Globalization on Trial: Crisis and Class Struggle in East Asia," *Monthly Review* 50/4 (September 1998).

172. Hart-Landsberg, "From the Claw to the Lion," 15.

173. Gao, *The Battle for China's Past: Mao and the Cultural Revolution,* 188–89.

Index